SOPHIE SHERWIN

There's Always a Hitch

A Daughter's Journey through her Mother's Footsteps

Copyright © 2019 by Sophie Sherwin

All rights reserved. No part of this publication may be reproduced, stored or transmitted in any form or by any means, electronic, mechanical, photocopying, recording, scanning, or otherwise without written permission from the publisher. It is illegal to copy this book, post it to a website, or distribute it by any other means without permission.

Sophie Sherwin asserts the moral right to be identified as the author of this work.

Second edition

ISBN: 978-1-06-862410-0

This book was professionally typeset on Reedsy. Find out more at reedsy.com

This book is dedicated to Mum

Mum – I love you and miss you with every inch of my soul and every moment of my life. Thank you for being you and for teaching me to be proud of who I am today, foibles and all.

NEVER GIVE UP

Contents

Foreword	ii
Well, Hello There and Welcome	1
Disclosure	7
Bon Voyage…Into the Unknown	9
Furry Couch Anyone?	16
My Snobbiness is Ebbing Away!	26
Dahlings… I Am Here for My Scene!	34
Something Straight Out of a Disney Movie	44
Viva Las Vegas	55
How Come My Arse is Growing at the Same Speed My Bank…	69
San Diego – My Paradise!	78
Meltdown	87
My Mum – My Hero	95
Long Beach Part Deux	101
Shenanigans on Catalina Island	107
Whistle Stop Tour of San Francisco	120
Journey from Hell	131
Seattle – Signs Are Everywhere	139
Vancouver – The Beginning of the End	151
I Fucking Made it!	163
What Happened Next	173
Thank You	179

Foreword

"Thanks to Sophie for writing this tribute to Annabella and the adventures we had in 1958.

Annabella was very special, and we remained lifelong and affectionate friends.

We started to holiday together in our senior years (albeit more sedately).
She is always in my heart."

Gerrie Hornsby (nee McLaughlin)
1959 - 2023

Well, Hello There and Welcome

Life is an adventure – you create your own. You can just engage in adventures or people decide to be adventurers. My mum chose both.

This is a story about three brave teenagers in the 1950s, who go hitchhiking with backpacks around the United States and Canada as told by my mum and Gerrie. But also, little did I know that I followed in my mum's footsteps and have found myself living an adventurous life and creating my own adventures.

I am currently sitting in LA, a little like mum, not a lot of cash in my pocket but getting caught up in the lights, opportunities and probably worse smog than back in the 50s, mixed with the aroma of marijuana.

I want to introduce my mum – Annabella Bisiker 'Bella'. She was born into an English middle class, comfortable family with dogs, a love of horses and an adventurous, cheeky spirit with a wicked sense of humour. Sadly, she passed away 11 years ago, but it has always been in me to write her incredible story and to live her legacy.

The other two adventurers you will get to know more later, but for now, let me acquaint you with Gerrie who was, a confident, energetic, funny, kind, opinionated brunette beauty with a love of travelling. The other adventurer is the shyest of the three; Janet, and as said by the others as 'not the brightest tool in the box' but with a vivacious, curious, fun and sociable personality to make up the threesome. *

It was a huge inconvenience to her; this attention seeking, pukey, loud bundle had come and upset the balance, and she had no control over it… However, she thought she could control parts of her life. A few weeks after he was born, she had decided that she had had enough of him getting all the attention. Clearly it was because he was a boy, so she told everyone she was going to be called Keith. For six weeks she did not answer to anyone who called her by her name, but only to Keith. This, as you can imagine, did not go down too well with her parents and teachers at school. She hung onto her stubbornness for as long as she could but eventually gave up grudgingly.

This did not work, so she thought of another tactic. If she could not get the attention away from this snot making machine, then she would get 'it' away from her and her mum. She went to the post office to put a sign in the window which read along the lines of,

'For sale–my brother… Wanted – a pony!'

Sadly, this idea did not quite work either, as the owner of the shop called her parents to let them know where she was – plan foiled! She was certainly an out-of-the-box thinker… Which is probably where I get it from and have only now just started to celebrate and embrace.

The story that I am going to share with you as mentioned, is about the travels and adventures of these three girls. I will also be sharing my adventures. Who knew that my life would turn out the way it has and that I have been fortunate to share the same spirit as my mum, so I can be on a journey physically, emotionally and spiritually, and share it with you.

Why read this book? It will hopefully inspire your inner adventurer but also will show you to not hold back if you want to do something. It is a story of friendship, enormous bravery, women's empowerment, life and snippets into the lives of young women in the 1950s, navigating life and learning about themselves. How best to do that is to take themselves out of their comfort zone and into situations which sometimes got dicey.

Life back then was either simpler or more complicated, depending on whether you had money or not. I think the three of them represented different backgrounds and childhoods nicely. The 1950s were dominated by women using their sexuality to get men's attention – think Marilyn Monroe, Audrey Hepburn, Elizabeth Taylor. Mum, Gerrie and Janet used theirs too, in the journey to get rides, meals and even hotel and hostel stays, in addition to the generosity from people who loved their story and adventure and would happily 'donate' towards it. This was in the form of winks, nudges, showing a little bit of leg, and flirting.

Have you ever done something that you think is a great idea at the time but then think, "Umm...? Why?" This is what happened when the girls excitedly went into the town of Banff and bought their backpacks. They were very naïve and bought big ones thinking like 'girls'; the bigger the pack, the more stuff they can take! Little did they know they would come to regret that decision. They spent a few weeks with sore backs and if the wind blew too hard, they would have fallen over. I am sure they experienced disjointed hips and moodiness due to an overbearing load until they met Mr Magic in the form of a scout leader in California, who showed them how to wear the packs correctly… I think it was one of many 'blonde' moments.

I, myself am experiencing this right now on my journey; when I left on my travels to the US, I packed far too much. I am such a 'just in case' packer and admire anyone who can pack lightly. I thought I was doing well with two weekend bags and one suitcase! However, since I have been here, I think my bags must sit in a grow bag overnight as I seem to now have five. How does that happen? It is not easy to move around with such a load, but I certainly know how the girls felt having to lug all that luggage around – thanks mum spirit (said raising my eyes to the sky). I don't have to go through EVERYTHING you experienced!

The girls also mention a few times that they were incredibly fortunate by the hospitality shown by everyone – they were not expectant and lived every moment, not worrying about the next day. This is what I am truly trying to accomplish myself. I have always been a planner, someone with an innate need to control everything, a perfectionist, I make decisions based from fear and most importantly for me – needing roots. Material stuff gives me comfort and safety and I am trying to find a community. This will be one big learning lesson!

Now, I guess a little about me – the star of the show? Not sure….I describe myself as a wine-loving, Jack of all trades and a master of none. However, the mastery I do have and use, is humour. It comes naturally to me which you will see throughout this book (well, I bloody hope so!) This is where mum and I were very similar – we both liked to joke and see the funny side in situations. In addition, we are both also very kind and generous. My journey is not so much about friendship but more about discovering my destiny, facing fear head on, learning to live a completely different way to my comfort zone, learning to live without, resilience, laughter and tears, and I am sure there was blood too, and it wasn't even mine.

How did I get here? Writing this book? I haven't a fucking clue! kidding… Mum used to regale the stories of her travels and I remember once she showed me her diaries and scrapbooks she had kept. It has been simmering for a few months, thinking her story should be shared, then one day this year, I woke up and thought, "I want to find those diaries."

They had been sitting in my brother's garage for over ten years and I was not even sure if they were in any kind of condition. Luckily, they were, and that is when it all began. Rewind a little more back to January 2018, I made up my mind to leave my job and embark on the entrepreneurial road, which has been a bit of a disaster. I have a lot of experience and skills I can use, and good qualifications, but not a lot of self-belief. In addition, I had quite a lot of money behind me but sadly I have lost it all by investing in people and companies who only care about money themselves. One huge message we get is 'invest in yourself ', well, that is what I did but frustratingly, in the wrong ones. They wrap their promises up in a beautiful bow and I got caught up in the 'sell'. So, I am making this journey with the few scraps of savings I have left.

Rewind even more to my background. I was brought up in a wealthy area in a large house and we never went without. I have spent most of my adult life with money, earning well and having a lifestyle to match. I now live with having to watch every dime I spend, and I cannot remember the last time I went on a shopping spree, but I am determined to do this journey.

Those diaries and scrapbooks were a gift to me. When I was given them, I did not know what to do with them but now I do; fulfil my destiny.

* Janet's name has been changed as the original third adventurer. I was not given consent to have her name printed and published.

Disclosure

First off – there is a whole lot of swearing in this book. If you are of the faint-hearted genre, then skip over those bits!

All the opinions expressed are mine or mums, and Gerrie's gets squeezed in too. I am not perfect and may offend people but there is absolutely no intention of doing so. Some parts have been embellished for entertainment purposes so please do not take me too seriously. This book has an aim to make you laugh, giggle, cry and realise that although this trip appears to be one disaster after another – I had fun making it. I saw parts of the world I would not have chosen to if mum had not taken me, and I would not have met some of the people I did or learnt the lessons I have.

I have no affiliation with any of the companies I have mentioned, and I do not advocate people to try or not try them. It is completely your choice and they were my experience at the time.

This book may not be your cup of tea and that is okay. That is the great thing about freedom of choice. For those who love this book and have learnt something then, big love to you.

In the book I talk of and mention stuff about signs and spirituality. These are my beliefs. Everyone has different thoughts but mine keep me going in the times I just want to give up. They bring me comfort, tears and giggles. I do not preach them to anyone but if you want to know more, then cool.

Bon Voyage…Into the Unknown

As mum sat there in her bedroom, fussing over her favourite being, her dog Quita, frustrated after another run-in with her dad, her mind wandered to her upcoming trip and excitement settled her. Her mind wandered to where she was going and the travel to get there. Ticket booked - £63.00, for a seven-day sail starting from the 1st of November 1957, in Liverpool and docking in Montreal, then getting to Toronto to begin her new life.

Her decision to leave a comfortable life in a small town in the North of England was a momentous one. She had just started a job as a stenographer after finishing her training, but she yearned for more. She felt trapped in this small town as it had no 'life' or excitement, and this highlighted the boredom. There was a whole, huge world out there and mum was determined to see it, feel it, experience it and defy 'expectations' of women her age at that period in time. She allowed her feelings of wonderment and the anticipation of possibilities and opportunities to sit and a huge smile came to her face.

Her choice to leave was an easy one but not without fear. The reason why her parents let her go was because she was going to stay with family in Toronto so there was a safety net for her. This appeased her parents, and certainly her mum fully supported her decision to travel across the world. Her dad was a little relieved for this ball of energy to be put to use but did not say an awful lot about it. He was not the most communicative, warm person and he and mum clashed a lot.

Her father was a strict accountant who wanted her to have a good job then find someone with whom to settle down. She adored her mum, Pinkie, who was her rock, best friend, comfort and biggest cheerleader. They were very close and would be her sounding board when she was having angst with her father. She would miss her desperately, but she was encouraged to leap into the unknown and experience the world. Of course, her mum would worry but she knew Bella was feisty and 'no' was not really a word in her vocabulary. Even if she heard the word, she would have selective deafness as you will see throughout this book. Mum had seen this freedom of travel and adventure through her aunts who were like a second mother to her, one of them especially; Eileen. She was lucky to have very strong females in her life which fueled her inner strength and courage.

The night before she left, she had a 'last supper' with her mum and dad. She was sitting at her dressing table when her dad walked in with his camera saying, "Photo, photo!" He took a photo of her, capturing the emotions on her face through a huge smile and poise, and then went into his bedroom to encapsulate the emotions of Pinkie, whose face showed the sadness, worry and heartache for her little girl going off on her own. Despite her feelings, they went and had dinner, and again a photo was taken to capture this big event.

Mum woke up the next day bursting with excitement and trepidation. She said her goodbyes to her housekeeper, and then to her brother by telephone, before they set off to Liverpool. Saying goodbye to her mum was the hardest thing she had ever done, and she had the sudden fear of 'what if it doesn't work?' Drying the tears, she embarked The Empress and waved goodbye madly from the deck, as her parents, dog and the land became smaller and smaller.

The journey was thoroughly enjoyable. She shared a cabin with three other girls and they certainly engaged in 'life on board'. They also made many other friends who were passengers and crew, so she did not have the time to miss home too much, yet. Of course, she did have her heart filled with how much she missed her mum and Quita.

Her cabin, C1, was compact but adequate and she had the bottom bunk. Luckily, she had enough space for all of her luggage. Once she unpacked, it became home for the next six days. She took part in quizzes, treasure hunts, games, social activities and a spectacular gala. The journey went quickly, and she had a ball. She was in her element being able to attend lots of parties, and she thought if this is how it is going to be in Canada, she had certainly made the right decision.

Once she got to Toronto, she stayed with family before going to live in a place called Fudger House. It was owned by Mr Fudger who ran a department store and he wanted his female staff to have a home away from home, so he opened this home for young business ladies from all over the world. They did not have to work at the department store – mum didn't, she worked in an office in Toronto for The Imperial Life Assurance Company of Canada. They did have to apply to stay there, however, as it was quite a prestigious place! There were no rules, 'only those essential to the well-being of group life'.

Mum's Diary Entry Whilst Working in Banff - Summer 1958

While I was working in Toronto as a stenographer, I decided to try for a job at a famous hotel in Banff in the heart of the Rockies which only opens for the Summer. The hotel replied to say that the only vacancy was as a chambermaid, I was a little dismayed at this as I had always worked in an office (this was a bit of a comeback), however, I decided to go along to the housekeeper who was in Toronto interviewing people. She painted a very bleak picture of long hours and 14 rooms a day and advised me to think about it for a day or two. That evening I discussed it with my friends who told me that thousands of students take summer jobs doing anything they can get and that I was lucky to get the chance of any kind of job in such a beautiful place. Combined with the fact that the hotel paid my return fare out I finally made up my mind to go.

Mum was never one to give up – she was so disappointed that she got turned down for the office job, but that was not going to stop her. She wanted more adventure than her life in Toronto.

I set out in the middle of May on the three-day train journey out to Banff. It was an interesting journey seeing the changing scenery. First the lakes in North Ontario then the flat prairie land of Saskatchewan, where finally we reached Calgary. We had our first glimpse of the Rockies in the distance. I had to get up very early to ensure a seat in the domed roof carriage, so that I would get a good view of the mountains.

When we finally arrived at the hotel the first thing was to be assigned to a room. I found myself sharing with two waitresses, both university students, in a tiny room just big enough to squeeze in three beds and a set of drawers. All we had for our clothes was one drawer each so the rest we kept under our beds. Not the ideal place for clean clothes! I found I was to work on the seventh floor with eight other girls, none of whom knew any more than I did. We were each given 14 rooms to do a day with,

1. *Three of the girls as reserves to help whoever was the busiest,*
2. *One girl as a reserve to help two others.*

Each girl would give her reserve a third of the tips so that everyone got two thirds. At first the hotel wasn't full, so we only had an average of six rooms a day. This took us all our time so that we were quite sure. We should never do 14 but once we got into a routine we soon speeded up. At the beginning of the season we had several conventions which were large groups of businessmen, sometimes with their wives sometimes without, who came supposedly to discuss business but who seemed to spend most of their time at parties and banquets. These conventions were not at all popular with the staff as they usually left a block tip which when shared out amongst 900 staff, left very little for each person.

One convention in particular, I remember there were around 600 men without their wives. After the first day all chambermaids had to go into the rooms in twos. Sometimes when the wives were included in the conventions, they would all be presented with orchid sprays. When they left, they would give them to us and I am sure new guests must have thought it rather a funny sight, dusty chambermaids wearing expensive orchid sprays. During the day we would wear blue overalls with white aprons rather like nurses, topped off with the most ridiculous caps you can imagine. They were pieces of white material, which when folded in a certain way, they were supposed to stand up. If they had been properly starched they might have, but they flopped all over the place. After much experimenting I folded mine into a flat square and pinned it down so that it looked like a pancake on my head. I always felt very self- conscious and wished I could have lost it without anyone noticing.

Mum was delighted when Princess Margaret went to stay in the hotel as part of her Canadian tour back in July 1958. It was a military operation with much security detail, and the staff had strict instructions on how to behave and the goings on. She saved a lot of memorabilia for her scrapbook.

Mum and Gerrie both loved to travel on their days off.

Our free day, or day off, we utilised to see the beauty spots and places of interest in Alberto. We found out very soon upon our arrival that almost everyone was using the method of hitchhiking as a means of seeing the spots of interest.

Gerrie and Janet casually invited mum to join them on a trip which they intended to make at the end of the season. She accepted just as casually.

We had had phenomenal luck with our hitchhiking in Canada. Would it be possible to do it in the US? We decided to chance it together.

01st September 2019

I came to LA in January and loved it – it was a little cold and I was not prepared for the issue of homelessness, which still shocks me today. Due to the location of where I was staying, I really was not able to indulge in life here, but I had a snippet and I wanted more. I am now back... With a new vigor, sunscreen and huge expectations.

Rewind to the reason I came back. I had to leave Vienna where I was living, and I had three months to figure out where I was going. Nothing was keeping me there, not even my disastrous dating life!

The clock was ticking, and I really did not know where to go. The most obvious decision was to go back to London, but I really did not want to... Pondering until someone asked me where I would love to go if I could, and I said straight away – LA. The next day, I booked my ticket, booked the movers and advertised some stuff I wanted to sell. Packing proved tricky as I did not know what I was going to be doing. I wanted to pack for all eventualities – and boy, did I do that. One suitcase, two weekend bags and over fifty kilograms later, I was on my flight! Fear, excitement, with a really annoying woman who would not stop talking, took over as the plane left Austria to a new adventure and the complete unknown. The only solid 'plan' I had was that I had a landing pad when I arrived. Other than that, I was putting my hands in the universe. I was going to write the book sitting in LA in a comfortable flat in a nice area, attending parties.

Furry Couch Anyone?

Back in 1958, September 18th, an invitation arrives under the door addressed to Room 1056.

"You are invited to THE farewell 'do'(Charleston) in 1036 tonight! Of course, IF you can't come, we'll understand perfectly. Just don't expect your money back, that's all!

Arrive promptly at nine thirty – leave when you like!

It must be clearly understood, however, that if you haven't left by nine tomorrow, you WILL be chucked out!

The Flappers!!!"

The summer was coming to the end in Banff, the endless round of parties, steak roasts, mountain hikes and other activities ended. The day before the hotel was closing, mum, Gerrie and Janet hitched into Banff to get their supplies for their upcoming adventures. They spent $24 on sleeping bags and a rucksack each. They each had saved up as much as they could ranging from $320 to $230. They spend the last night full of excitement and trepidation.

Mid-September 2019

Three weeks into my LA adventure and it certainly has been a roller coaster so far, including having been talked down from the cliff edge of self- doubt about my ability to write this book and my debilitating fears of money.

You see, I am doing this trip on a budget AND without a car - yeah, yeah… I cannot quite figure out which is harder – having only a few dollars or having to rely on my legs and/or public transport to get around. So, my landing pad when I arrived certainly threw me into the realisation of why you need a car (or it just makes your life so much easier) here in LA. Boy, was I so incredibly fortunate that I had found myself living in a gated community in a gorgeous house with a swimming pool, I thought I had won the lottery… Until I realised it must be a place where people go to die or get sober. Neither were in my plan! It is in the Hollywood Hills and unless you are rich enough to have a driver, you really must have a car. I even tried alternative methods when I was there – public transport – but the nearest bus stop is a 30-minute walk down a very steep hill in the searing heat, the buses only come every 20 minutes, and there is no shade at the bus stop, so that did not really work out. The second option was to call an Uber; well, that was laughable – it takes hours for one to come, so you would get to your destination and then have to turn around to come back again – bloody useless. I had to rely on my friend to give me a lift and then I would get an Uber back. I hear you say – why didn't I hire a car? Well, remember I am on a budget and paying for Uber was not really in my plan either.

I spent those two weeks in virtual isolation. One of my goals was to get out there and meet people but I came to realise that was not the universe's goal for me at the start. I did go to a three-day event, which was to learn more about the way we tick and our businesses, but it did not go so well. It turns out that people are incredibly rude and unwelcoming when they feel threatened by a newbie. I was ignored by some people for the whole event and judged by others.

That is all I can really say about that, but it did leave a nasty taste in my mouth and it was the start of the walk up the cliff of self-doubt. It also renewed my knowing that people can be full of shit and promise you things that don't materialise.

I was offered a ticket out of isolation, into town, and a couch to sleep on, so I thought it was perfect as I could then begin my LA 'life' and really experience and see where mum had been. I packed my suitcase (ha ha – suitcase – I really do not understand how my luggage grows overnight, so I have more like a whole consignment with me suddenly), said goodbye to my friend and headed off to the next chapter.

Well now… What can I say? How can I put this as politely as possible? I ended up in a shit hole. I have seen and lived with boys who are not the cleanest, so I could maybe – on a good day and if that was the only problem – have looked past the cleanliness. After I walked in the door, I put my bags down and he gave me a tour. First stop was the kitchen. He asked if I cook, I looked at him awkwardly and said 'yes', thinking about my bag of organic quinoa, cold- pressed organic olive oil and vegetables in my bag. He said I would have to cook in the microwave as the gas cooker was not hooked up yet. He went on to say that he usually eats out, so he has not had a need for the appliance. He then told me that he would get more cutlery and plates etc. I didn't think anything of it until later when I went back to the kitchen…

We moved into the bathroom, where he pulled back the shower curtain and pointed out that the only ventilation is the broken window that overlooks the parking lot, so it is best to keep it closed when showering and when peeing on the toilet. I have to make sure the shower curtain is pulled all the way otherwise the locals will have a free show every day! Mortification… I was trying not to look too hard at the cob-webs, dust and damp, and eagerly moved on. hell to the no – he does not have one.

He showed me his wardrobe and hanging area but did not offer to allow me to hang anything, so I asked casually if he had an iron. I can work around living from a suitcase, but I really do need to iron some clothes, but of course Then we went back to where I would be sleeping – the living room, on the couch. He casually mentioned that there is no Wi- Fi… Hold up… WHAT the FUCK? Okay, don't panic I thought, there is a TV. I asked if it worked, and he said no… Oh shit… My life is ebbing away! (I am a TV addict, and it helps me switch off). He told me I could hotspot the internet off my phone, so I needed to go and get unlimited data… I stopped listening to anything else really after that as he was going on about windows and his cat, the air conditioning, the key, the neighbourhood… Blah blah – my mind was still on the NO WIFI. Houston, we have a problem… What am I supposed to do? I run a business from home. At this point, I was really trying to hold back the tears or stopping my hands from finding their way around this person's throat… I did have to laugh though – he asked me to please not put the cushions on the floor as they might get dirty when I turn the sofa into a bed. I think I actually snorted with laughter.

I mentioned a cat earlier – this was a gorgeous cat, but it was long haired and white and grey – well, you can imagine, the dark blue couch was fur-lined. I honestly didn't think this place, or the couch had seen cleaning materials for at least this century. I was in shear panic mode but thought I was saving money here as it was cheap… Try it out and see… Nope, I lasted less than 48 hours!

He had not had a spare key cut, so I could not leave my valuables when I went out, which was for most of the day. I had to carry nearly everything with me, so I felt like a homeless person with all my belongings… He kept saying it was a safe area, but he had in fact only been there a month. I certainly did not feel too safe.

In those 40 - something hours, I went back to explore in the kitchen to discover hidden treasures – which were zero. Honestly, there was one plate and three wine glasses. That was it. He really did eat out. So, it was cake for me and a lot of wine. I must also mention about the night's sleep or lack thereof I had. This place was near a hospital which happens to have a helipad on top and the flat is under it – do I need to go on? The Wi-Fi issue was a no - go, and I just could not stay there so I found myself an emergency Airbnb and off I went.

Mum's adventure seemed to begin in a plume of drama too!

September 24th 1958

Up at 7.15 for our last beanery breakfast. Sat on one of the middle tables. Took grapefruit and sugar for the journey. Said goodbye to Mrs Frihaganand Joan and Lucy. Back in our room we finished packing our haversacks and cleaned up the room. We each have haversacks, sleeping bags and either hand grylls or a bucketbag. The haversacks are far heavier than we anticipated. We could hardly get them on. We were ready at about 09.30 and accumulated everything outside the upper annex where Alf took some photos of us. We said a last 'goodbye' to Mrs Douglas and Mrs Frihagan. It was a beautiful clear sunny morning though very cold. Alf put a quarter in Janet's 'curse cup' when he said goodbye. There was an American lady nearby who took the hint and gave Janet a silver dollar good luck piece (luckily it didn't go in because the box was later lost but they still had the luck silver dollar). We waited for the truck which took the trunks down to the station and got a lift down. Gerrie went right to the station and Janet and I stopped off at the post office to post numerous parcels. We walked to the station and just arrived as the Dominion was pulling out. I was very sorry to miss it.

Outside the station we hitched, and the first car stopped. It was Glenn, a park warden. He said he was going to Eisenhower Junction via Johnsons Canyon. We decided we would like to see Johnson's Canyon, so we went along too. He said he would be about an hour. We walked quite away but not right to the canyon as we were afraid we would miss Glenn. However, we had to wait an hour, we thought he had forgotten us. When he eventually came, he said he would take us to Golden as he was on holiday. We thought this was fine, however, he stopped seemingly at every warden's cottage for a chat and a drink. At one place, Wapta Lodge, he said he would be an hour.

Three hours later we decided to go and look for him. We spent the next two hours in front of an enormous log fire. We had coffee and cookies and looked at magazines. We were a bit dubious about continuing with Glenn as he was pretty drunk but there was hardly any traffic, so we decided to chance it. It was an extremely hair-raising journey as he was swerving all over the road, but we kept him awake by talking to him and getting him to sing Western songs to us. He had quite a nice voice. We arrived in Golden at about 9.00pm *where we had Western sandwiches. Glenn called a policeman friend of his over to see if he could help with accommodation. We secretly hoped he would say we could sleep in the prison but no such luck. Glenn found us a motel for two, so I sneaked in after. We paid $5.00. He took quite a long time to go but eventually left at 11.00. Gerrie slept on the floor in a sleeping bag and Janet and I in the double bed. Gerrie doesn't like sleeping with other people. So ends our first day on the road. It has certainly been pretty eventful even if we didn't get very far (110 miles).*

September 25th 1958

I was the first to wake so I went and got the shopping for breakfast. It was quite a thrill being the little housewife for once. We had oranges, cereal, cheese on toast and coffee. Most of it was Beanery food. I had to nip into the shower room when the owner called in about the sheets. We got onto the road again at about 11.00. There was a train from Golden to Revelstoke at 2.00 which cut out the 'big bend' so we thought if we didn't get a lift by then we would catch it. However, the first car we hitched was going right round. He was a little French Swiss man called Andre Schumacher. He was very helpful and piled everything he could in the trunk.

We set off on one of the worst rides I hope we ever have. 200 miles of potholes, trenches of mud and dust. We could only do an average of 30 – 35 mph. On the way we had a flat tire. It was very funny to watch Andre change it as he is rather effeminate and had never done one before. Luckily, he had a spare tire and there was very little other traffic. He was the man who should have given Erica a lift to Vancouver, but she got fed up of waiting and went on. I remember seeing him peeping through the curtains of the Timberline when I went up to collect the money for my pass.

We had lunch at a little wayside restaurant at about 3.00pm. It was nice scenery though the mountains weren't as impressive as in Banff. It was interesting coming to the enormous trees of BC. They towered over us on each side of the road. We had long discussions with Andre about marriage, women and various races. He made no bones about the women he had had nor the fact that he was going to advertise for a wife.

We had a coffee at another small transport café at 8.00pm when it was dark. We arrived in Revelstoke at 10.00 pm where we had a tomato juice in a beer parlour. Then we carried on to Vernon, another 90 miles. He got us in a very post Auto Court for $8, we paid $2 each and he paid the rest. We eventually got into bed at about 2.00am after a very tiring day.

September 26th 1958

Gerrie and I got up to do the shopping. We hitched to a grocery store and walked back. Vernon seemed a lovely little peaceful county place after Golden, which was a god-forsaken shack town. We had just finished breakfast at 11.00am when Andre came in. He was going into the town, so we packed hurriedly and went with him. He did some business while we looked for jobs either picking or packing apples. We had no luck, so Andre drove us on to Kelowna. On the way we stopped at a factory in Oyama, but no luck. It was another beautiful sunny day. We ran most of the way along by the Okanagan Lake. We went through several orchards, but it still seemed rather barren in places. We arrived in Kelowna for tea. We were going to pay but Andre joined us and paid. We tried a few more factories but still no luck, so he found us a motel. He did a little more bargaining for us and paid the extra $1 out of the $7. We did some shopping whilst he went off then cooked him an egg, toast, *coffee and fruit dessert. It took three of us half an hour!*

The motel owner was the silliest, most ignorant man I have met. He had too much saliva and kept saying, 'I'm just joshing you!' when he made a silly remark. We said goodbye to Andre as he was going on. He was very good to us, but we didn't really like him! We went to bed pretty early.

September 27th 1958

Up quite early and cooked breakfast. Just as we were leaving the motel Andre appeared. We were so surprised to see him that we sort of brushed him off when he offered to take us round the orchards. We didn't want to impose on him anymore. We didn't see him again after that and felt a bit guilty.

We hitched out to the mission and then walked a little way to the orchards. We wandered around for an hour but still couldn't get a job. It was so lovely there with the orchards reaching down to the blue Okanagan Lake and hills beyond. There was such a peaceful air as well. We returned to the mission at 11.00am to meet a man with whom we had had a lift off. He said he may be able to help us, but he didn't come. There was a home bake sale at the mission, so we went on a bus and bought an apple crumble tart. We got a lift back in a toast master van which was good fun. He gave us a packet of cakes to eat. We just got back at 12.00pm when we had to vacate the motel but decided to stay on another night. We spent the afternoon sunbathing on the lawn in front of the motel.

At 4.00pm Gerrie and I did the shopping for supper and breakfast. We had a hurried supper and then hitched out to the mission once more. We took a little walk up to the orchards in the dark and picked about a dozen apples each! I stuffed mine up my front. I felt awful walking along without a ring. Our private apple picking jaunt was very successful! We went to bed quite early again!

My Snobbiness is Ebbing Away!

17th September 2019

We all know that Airbnb owners wouldn't know the truth if it hit them in the arse and that the description is a crock of shit. I am learning that more and more. I am also learning my once high standards have dramatically dropped. My snobbiness is ebbing away. I happen to have spent a lot of time and money on Airbnb's, and the more I do the worse it seems to get. I think homeowners just want to rip people off, for us to pay their rent or mortgage. So, can you feel my excitement building for my living arrangements?

I arrive at this apartment and I have read the description very, very carefully. I cannot imagine what can go wrong… Oh boy – here we go again. Does no one in LA own a duster or know how to clean properly? Clearly not, but honestly, I was so glad to get out of the last place and see a working gas cooker, plates and a normal kitchen, that I was overlooking the dust… I am introduced to their dog, who is super cute and energetic. He is mentioned in the ad and I was told that he would not be a problem – all good.

I start unpacking, look around my bedroom and realise that I am on a mezzanine level. I notice that the wall stops halfway up to the ceiling, so I have physical privacy but no noise privacy. I get to hear everything in the kitchen, when the front door opens, and oh the quiet dog?? Not so quiet – he barks the whole time the owners are not there! REALLY?I have a call that evening with my mentor and she talks me back down from another cliff edge of sheer panic… I am honestly ready to give up and leave LA… I am also having a major panic attack about money. The fear of money is horrific – so if you have ever experienced it – boy, am I with you… My mentor told me to go out there and do things, start having fun – FUN? What the hell is that? I had not had it for a while, so yes, I thought – and that, ladies and gentlemen is where my story really begins…

18th September 2019

The next day, I pulled my big girl pants on and decided to do some writing for the book but also to do what I love, and people watch. Hollywood is certainly the best place for that! You get all sorts of people from around the globe and all walks of life… So, off I trotted to Hollywood.

I settled down in Starbucks and got down to some serious writing. Jazz was playing in the background along with the hum of chatter. Others were quietly sitting and looking at their phones or reading, and of course the mass of laptops. Now and again a homeless person came in and sat down but no one seemed to bat an eyelid. They did not stay for long.

After a while I was distracted by a woman who sat down opposite me and announced to the two gentlemen who were sitting next to me that she had just seen a dead body. Well, of course I couldn't concentrate on what I was doing, so I listened under the guise that I was thinking. The conversation then ensued about how many dead bodies each of these people had seen – it is apparently a 'thing' which I did not know. Awful but intriguing. It got me pondering about the dead bodies I have seen... Not exactly what I expected to be thinking about!

The gentlemen eventually left, and the woman swooped next to where I was sitting and started a conversation with me. I was just about to tell her my experiences about dead bodies, but she instead took a darker twist and told me about a rape she experienced back in the 70's and that she was not traumatised by it, contrary to what people said. It completely threw me, and I really did not want to continue the conversation, but she kept going. Whilst she was talking, she was eating a sandwich and luckily for me, she did not take too long to finish it before leaving. It then got me thinking about how open she was about this traumatic experience. On the one hand, I thought it was great that it was out in the open and not some dirty little secret, but on the other hand, I was uncomfortable... I did a little work after that, but not much, so I stopped writing and left. I was exhausted, so I went back to my 'digs', watched TV and fell asleep.

19th September 2019

After a good night's sleep, I was super excited as I was having my hair done and it was costing next to nothing. I also decided to ask a Facebook group if anyone knew of a walk-in acting class I could attend (I am in LA, right?). People were very good and responded, so I would put that to the side and deal with it later. I went to the hair appointment, but unfortunately it did not work out and I was bummed, so I thought I would run an errand instead. On my way, I came across this shocking banner which was part of a free museum called 'Psychiatry: An Industry of Death'. Two and a half hours later, I emerged blinking into the sunshine. It was so fascinating, sad and shocking, but I felt good that I had educated myself a little more about the way the world works.

I continued to run my errands but to no avail, as I could not find what I was looking for. I decided I was pretty famished, so I went to a famous hotdog stand. The line was long, and the sun was strong, but I was determined to stay and try them. The most famous hotdog is a Chilli Cheese Dog, which literally is plastic cheese on a bun with what looks like 'a shop bought' hotdog, onions and mincemeat. It looked so unappetising that I just could not bring myself to eat it, so I opted for a Chicago Polish something. Was it worth it? Hell no, along with all the other touristy stuff that is overpriced… But at least I can take that off my bucket list (it was never on there to be honest, but I know not to waste ink putting it on there). I left… Stuffed but underwhelmed.

I was planning to have a quiet night in, however, I wanted to pop to the supermarket to get some supplies (I think it was a bottle of wine…) On my way home, I came across this tiny theatre which was advertising an improv comedy show on Saturday night. I quite fancied going, so I went in to buy a ticket. There were people walking into a theatre room so I asked what was going on and would you believe it? It was an open acting class! The universe had seen my Facebook post! The teacher came out and asked if I was staying, I said that I was there to buy a ticket for the show on Saturday. She told me to buy the ticket and then come back to the class. So, I did!

I bought a ticket and then, I did my first acting class in LA!

I loved it… When we were going through acting the emotions, it was great as I could walk around shouting "fuck" at the top of my voice out of anger – the best therapy ever. It was a very long evening, but so worth it. I met some great people, showed off my acting skills, and got a thumbs up from the teacher. I left after signing up for more classes and a huge smile on my face! This inspired me to see what else I should do whilst in LA…

20th September 2019

Research on my book took me to Universal Studios. Again, it was very overpriced, and I walked away very underwhelmed… What was frustrating was that I wanted to see if I could stand on the same ground mum and the girls did. Unfortunately, everyone I spoke to, apart from one lady at the ticket office, was as unenthusiastic as a scarecrow on Mars by my story and not wanting to help me. I tried calling the PR woman and left a voicemail, but of course no returned phone call. As soon as I got there, I jumped on the same studio tour as mum had done, but it just felt like I was on a conveyor belt. Most of the lots were closed so you didn't really get to see much. The 3D experience was average and jaws jumping out of the water was like an underwhelming flaccid erection!

I think that the park is more focused on rides rather than showing the actual making of movies or TV shows, in which I am more interested. What I found fascinating was that mum caught the bus from their hotel and simply went in. Now, you must go by subway to the stop, walk a little, and then get a trolley bus to the entrance. After that there is a huge wait to get in… Oh, life seemed so much simpler back then! I went on a couple of rides, which satisfied my inner child, but the thought of queuing put me off the others. I did, however, buy the biggest doughnut from The Simpsons Land, of which I ate half for dinner and the other half the next day for breakfast. It was pretty delicious. I love any cake.

After Universal, I was feeling a little disappointed I wasn't being taken seriously, so I decided to go to a local bar and have a glass of wine. I was hoping for that 'All American' bar hospitality when you sit at the bar and you can tell the bartender all your problems. Then you walk away with either a sense that you must look into your drinking habits, or their phone number. Sadly, this did not happen, so I left after one glass.

October 13th 1958

We enquired at the travel desk about tours and booked one at 1.45pm for Hollywood and the studios. Then we went window shopping. A coach picked us up at the hotel and took us to the depot. There weren't many seats left so we were fairly near the back. I sat next to Janet and Gerrie sat behind. The driver was very nice and kept us amused all the time. He started off by telling all the women which side left and right were! Even then I got muddled! We went through Hollywood and around some of the stars' homes. Amongst them we saw Tennessee Ernie Ford's house. He was standing in his porch. Quite a thrill when he waved at the bus. We stopped at a soda fountain for ten minutes in Hollywood. Janet and I wandered around; it was quite thrilling being in Hollywood as you never know who you might see! Next, we carried on to the International Universal Studios.

When we entered the gates, a policeman gave us a brochure. It was really interesting, although we weren't allowed out of the bus. We saw all the false sets, the dressing rooms, even whole towns and made houses. It really was fascinating. We saw a glimpse of a film being made but didn't stop.

21st September 2019

The alarm was set for my next round of fun on Saturday which involved a 'cardio tap dancing' class. I was quite excited about it as when I was younger, I loved tap dancing. But as some of you know, you should leave certain things back in your childhood! It turns out it was National Dance Day and the instructor decided we should do a hip-hop routine in the form of tap. Well now… My tap career started that day and abruptly ended that day. I was the hottest mess amongst these wannabe Broadway stars. Instead of the lovely sound of pitter-patter of tap, it sounded like a stampede. But hey, it was fun, got me out of bed, and got my heart rate up enough to allow me to completely negate any burnt off calories by eating something sugary and delicious.

I then spent over an hour walking in the searing heat to a store, only to find that what I needed was sold out – it was almost comical. I jumped into an Uber home as I was completely exhausted.

That evening I went to the theatre to see the show that I had bought tickets for. It was a comedy improv show and it was so good. Directed by the wonderful Tim Simek and performed by 'Slow…Children at Play'. I think the actors were incredibly talented, being able to think quickly on their feet and be funny at the same time! Some of the jokes were a little lost on me as it was geared towards Americans, but that did not dent my enthusiasm and enjoyment.

The theatre itself was tiny, with only a few rows and about 30 seats – totally different from my usual theatre experience. I would love to go back when I am next in Noho.

22nd September 2019

Sunday is another eventful day. I decided to sign up to an afternoon/ evening of women empowerment. It was full of performers, speakers, dancers and people selling stuff. I thoroughly enjoyed meeting some people, especially a very talented artist whose work I very much liked. I was tempted to buy a piece, but sadly funds would not stretch and at this stage I don't have any walls on which to display it!

The highlight of the evening was going home. Sadly, even the overpriced bar wine was not enough for my enjoy-o-meter to be piqued. Don't get me wrong, some of the speakers were very inspiring, but the organisation was poor and most of the audience was clearly made up of friends and family. There was nothing new, which is what interests me and clearly the coaching world has managed to just spew out same old, same old speak.

The next couple of days came and went, I did not do too much.

Dahlings… I Am Here for My Scene!

25th September 2019

Wednesday was a very cool day. First of all, I went to have a look at a room in a house that I was interested in renting. On the way there, I had to ask a very nice man whether the bus I was waiting for was the correct bus, to which he replied it was. I am assuming upon hearing my English accent, he decided to start chatting to me. He was super nice and studying music at university. He gave me his card and asked if I wanted a tour of Noho, I should call him. I never did.

The landlady was so nice and had an incredible story. She was recovering from a brain injury after something fell on her head. Can you imagine that? She was so brave, and I really loved meeting her and having a good chat. She was so positive, using humour as part of her recovery. I knew we would have got on famously and her flat was just lovely, beautifully decorated and clean. I walked away with very positive vibes.

On the way back, I got talking to a vendor who was selling

coffee and food from a stall on the side of the road. It turned out that he was a very successful architect who wanted to open a restaurant. He had trained as a chef, so he had set up this stall as a challenge to make $25,000 by end of January to get the funding for his restaurant. He was not allowed to use any of his own money. I asked how it was going, and he confidently told me that he would reach his goal and more! Another fascinating story. I bought a piece of poppy-seeded lemon cake and it was amazing. In the evening, I went to a VIP screening of the movie 'Judy'. It was a story of Judy Garland's time in London a few months before she died. It was very powerful and sad. Due to being in the industry from such a young age, she had no friends. I guess it must be so tricky to trust people and she was not old enough to have established grounded and real friendships. I miss having people around me – it's one of the downsides of travelling alone. Yes, I get to speak to people, but it is all small talk. I fell into bed with a warm fuzzy feeling. I had a great day.

26th September 2019

The next day was just as good, I met with a new friend for coffee who has another very inspirational story. I met him because he was my Uber driver and we got talking and talking and talking. So, we decided to meet again; it was lovely to hang out with someone. I found this really cool coffee place called 'Republic of Pie' where I was able to sit and do some work before he turned up. We could have spent the whole evening chatting, but I had to go as my first real acting class was starting. I loved my acting class! I was one of three that night as others were unavailable to attend. I got to play a part in a scene and I, of course, wowed the audience of two people! Hey... You gotta start somewhere. I have resurrected my acting career... Hollywood, here I come!

27th September 2019

I woke up with the sun streaming, the dog barking, and the door slamming. Pissed off, I got up in a haze of expletives as I really wanted to sleep more. I decided to go to Downtown, which is affectionately known as DTLA. It is where mum and the girls stayed whilst here in LA, and my mission was to hunt down the hotels. I found that when I go on one of those jaunts, I get quite emotional. So, along with my emotions, I jump on the subway. I got off at Pershing Square, which is quite a well-known place and somewhere I know quite well.

I mentioned at the beginning of my part of the book that I had been to LA a few months prior. Well, I had in fact stayed in DTLA... I was reassured by a friend who had lived there that it was a great place. Well now, my back door was on Skid Row and the front door was one street away from Skid Row. For those of you who do not know what Skid Row is, it is a well- known place where the homeless live. When in London, I was used to seeing homelessness, but this was on a whole different level. The streets were littered with tents or people just sleeping on the floor, the litter and the smell, it can be quite overpowering. Most of the time we all coexist, but it was the people suffering from mental health and the drug takers who made me feel unsafe. I was spat at and verbally accosted by a couple of people, so, as mentioned, I did not really go out at night back in January. Aside from that, DTLA is improving. The developers have arrived and there are some great places to go, lovely restaurants, trendy coffee shops and a huge street food market which is very well known.

There was not enough room for me to pass so I was just trailing, in a complete world of my own. When I did manage to pass him, he flung out his arm and yelled at me to stop following him. If I had been any closer, he probably would have hit me...Welcome back to DTLA, I say to myself! I was a little shaken, so I sat and had a coffee to gather myself before I embarked on my mission. After a shot of caffeine, I walked down to the Barclay Hotel where mum and the girls stayed. There it was in all of its glory! Whilst walking along, looking down at the sidewalk, I thought that these were the very streets that mum had walked... It was incredible!

I went into the Barclay Hotel, and it looked like it had not changed since it was built. The walls and ceiling had a yellowy tinge from years of cigarette smoke and the musty smell was a mixture of old and of the people who had come and gone. It was now social housing. I approached the man behind the counter to ask about the history of the building. He was very helpful, friendly and excited by my story. He said that it was one of the best hotels back then – funnily enough mum had completely disagreed! She had said it was a 'dump' and I could see why. It was very surreal being there. The man also told me that Al Capone used to stay there and that there were tunnels underneath, which run around LA for the bootlegging, gun running, etc. Also, because of the prohibition, there were illegal, speakeasy bars in the tunnels. I checked this out and cannot confirm if there is a tunnel from the Barclay Hotel but there are tunnels. I said goodbye and went to the place they moved onto the second night, the Rosslyn Hotel – again the building and the sign outside was still there, but it had become social housing too. I went inside and it was beautiful. I spoke to the person behind the desk, but they were not as accommodating and excited as the manager in the Barclay Hotel. I asked if he knew if the décor was original, but he said he did not know. I said thanks and left.

It is very interesting how the universe synchronises. When I came to LA back in January, I mentioned that I had stayed downtown, and it turns out that I was two minutes away from the Barclay Hotel and the Rosslyn Hotel. I was dumbfounded when I noticed this. Who knew that I was pounding the same streets as mum, 60 years later and never knew! Exhausted, emotional, and elated, I jumped onto the subway and headed back home. Seems like mum and the girls had a better time.

October 12th 1958

It was with an elderly man who was going right into Los Angeles. He was very helpful and took us to the Y. When we got there, it was full. We were sitting in the lobby of the Y Hotel trying to decide what to do when three marines came up and started talking to us. They offered to find a cheap hotel for us to stay in. They found the Barclay Hotel then we returned to the Y. Two of the boys disappeared so Jim, Janet's Texan, got two others to help. Mine was a Mexican Texan, Victor, and was gorgeous! Really tall, dark and handsome.

The Barclay was a pretty crumby place but was only $2.00. The woman at the desk was a real b about the boys going up and told them they could only be a few minutes. When the boys were just leaving, she rang us to see if they had left. About a quarter of an hour later they rang and asked us if we would like to go and see a show. We said yes before I realised it was Sunday, then it was too late to back out. Even if I had remembered it would have been *a bit awkward. The lady at the desk apparently listened in. We met them in the lobby then walked along till we came to a suitable show. We saw 'Under Fire', 'Cowboy', and 'Pal Joey'. I had been looking forward to seeing 'Pal Joey' for ages. It was more or less a wrestling match with the other two, but Victor was just nice. We walked them back to the bus station as they had to be back at their base at midnight. The area we walked through was the worst I had ever been in. Two people offered to sell us stolen rings. We were scared stiff walking back. We went to bed when we got back. We were pretty disappointed with what we had seen of LA so far.*

October 13th 1958

We had the remains of Lea's picnic for breakfast. We decided we would go on a tour somewhere. We went down to check at the desk that we could stay on. The woman told us our room was taken and that all the others were taken. We didn't believe a word but there was nothing we could do about it. We were furious. We set off to look for another place and found the Rosslyn Hotel. It was $2.50 per night instead of $2.00 but we took it. It was situated on 5th and Main.

After Universal…

Then we returned to Downtown LA via the Hollywood Freeway. The LA Freeways are fabulous. We returned to our hotel at about 6 o'clock. The tour cost $4.35 and was well worth it. Janet and I went off to buy some fruit at a cheap stand Gerrie and I had found in the morning We decided we were hungry, or rather Janet was, so we went into a self- service restaurant. I was just hoping to watch, however when I got to the counter, I couldn't resist temptation and *bought myself a large steak and cheesecake! Hopeless! When we were in there, we saw a little old lady being taken away by a cop for not paying her bill. I wish I was a millionaire. We walked through Pershing Square where all the queers meet, homosexuals, religious fanatics etc. It seemed a shame as it was a lovely park with palm trees, etc. We decided we wanted to do a tour of the night clubs or at least go in one. The official tour was too expensive, so we dressed up and went on our own.*

We took a bus out to Hollywood to Grauman's Chinese Theatre. It is a fascinating place. All the most famous stars sign their names in concrete in front of the theatre and put their shoes and handprints on. Then we walked down Hollywood Blvd. it was almost deserted and hardly any nightclubs. We didn't find anywhere we thought suitable. Most disappointing. Up a little alleyway we saw a man who printed names on matches, etc. We decided to investigate. Gerrie had some matches done and I had four glass stands done. I had 'Douglas & Pinkie from Hollywood, California' written on. The man was very nice, and we spent about half an hour with him.

We walked down as far as Vine Street and went into the Brown Derby for coffee. It is a very well-known place. Then we caught a bus back to Pershing Square. We were walking down a street when we met a rather nice cop with a jolly smile. We got talking to him about LA, crime, etc. He showed us his truncheon and let me try it out. I took my shoes off after a bit. We must have looked pretty funny standing by the lights with our shoes off talking to a cop! After about an hour he hailed a couple of his friends in a cop car and asked them to give us a lift home. It was quite an experience!

The people in the lobby gave us queer looks when we arrived back! I forgot to mention that we called in at the Hollywood Rose Bowl at the end of our tour. It is a very famous outdoor theatre and was most interesting. I wanted to buy a present but didn't have the extra

2c for tax. This idea of adding on tax after really is annoying. So ends a really interesting day.

28th September 2019

Today I made a decision (well, the decision was made for me). Have you ever noticed with regards to situations that turn out just right, usually the path you take to get there is simple and easy, things just fall into place? I had spoken to the landlady I met a few days ago and said that I wanted to take the room, but I had to buy a bed. I found a cheap one and she kindly had arranged for one of her friends to help me move it. The day of moving the bed, it was the only day in all my time in LA that it was going to rain. The landlady's friends told me that the mattress may get wet and dirty as he only had an open truck… So, I said thanks but no thanks, I would find another solution but… This got me thinking…Was the universe telling me that I should leave LA and go on a journey? Fuck my fear… The decision was made, I was putting my hands in my destiny once again. I thought to myself, "Take all my stuff and travel, say goodbye to LA and comfort, and hello to all the places mum and the girls went to. Can I really do this?"

It was going to cost much more money, so I had to budget even more… No more organic quinoa or cold pressed olive oil… Instead it was supermarket crap. More of my snobbiness ebbing away.

Now, how to make my luggage easier to carry?! A second suitcase purchased and a bus ticket to Phoenix booked, I sat back and enjoyed my last couple of days in LA. I went for long, exploratory walks and on one of them, I saw this very long queue outside a bakery. Being terribly British, I had to join it. I asked the person in front of me if the bakery was famous for anything in particular, but apparently it wasn't. It was just well-liked by locals and people in LA. I queued for about 45 minutes and ordered a piece of carrot cake. OMG... It was the best I have EVER tasted. It was well worth the wait...

I also went back to Republic of Pie, which is cool. I learnt that it is a well-known coffee shop which specialises in, yup you guessed it... Pie, both sweet and savoury. I loved the place as all the conversations people were having were about films, TV shows, writing etc... I felt very 'at home' after my acting class! I also had to talk to the landlady to let her know that I was not moving in. She completely understood and said she thought it was the right thing for me to do.

October 14th 1958

Up fairly early. Gerrie and I went by bus to the main PO to see if there was any mail but no luck. When we got back the three of us set off for Ann and Bart's house. They were friends of Gerrie's sister in Toronto. It took us ages to get there. My watch had lost the glass and two of its hands, so I felt lost. We got halfway there, sat for 20 minutes waiting for the next one. We were all getting a bit short tempered with each other by then, when the bus finally came it wasn't going our way, so we hitched. We finally got there about 1.30pm. Ann and Bart are Norwegian and Havean 11-year old daughter, Marriette.

She came back from school about 4pm. Janet and I went for a walk while Gerrie helped Ann get the supper. We had chicken, rice, veggies, cherry tart and ice cream. Very good. Bart came home while we were still eating. He put up his movie projector and screen and we had a show after dinner. He had to go out again until about

10.30pm so we watched tv till he came home, then he drove us home.

Something Straight Out of a Disney Movie

01st October 2019

Bags packed; I headed off to the bus stop. I tried to be bright and breezy, chic and normal, but I looked anything but! I was pushing, grunting, swearing and completely uncoordinated, but I made it.

We all stood in this car park with the afternoon sun shining down wondering when the bus would arrive. It finally did and so I put my luggage in the underneath compartment and jumped on a bus headed to Phoenix. It was a great ride. We stopped in Palm Springs, which looked like a very nice place, and I got some lunch to eat back on the bus. I found the love of doughnuts here in the US amazing. You can get all flavours, shapes, sizes and variations. Seven hours later, two (ahem…) or four doughnuts later, I arrived in Phoenix.

Loaded with my bags, I started the next part of my journey to find my Airbnb. A very nice 'cop' helps me with directions to the light railway – I think he probably guessed that I was a tourist with my oversized luggage, pasty complexion, and with a clueless look on my face. Anyway, it was good to be pointed in the right direction, so I did not do my usual of walking around in circles trying to figure out in which direction Google Maps was pointing me.

I got on the light railway and it was taking me right to the corner of my road where I was staying for a few nights. Whilst on the tram car, this woman started singing at the top of her voice through her earphones to Barry White, far from sounding remotely like anyone who can sing. She sounded like she was being tortured, heavily… Non-stop. She had clearly been drinking as she was slurring and howling, entertaining commuters on their way home. I felt truly blessed to be serenaded as a welcome to Phoenix.

02nd October 2019

Phoenix proved disappointing. It was all too shiny and new, but I tried to look past that and enjoy what it had to offer. I ended up in the Wells Fargo museum. It was quite fascinating going through the history with supporting memorabilia. Excitedly, I spoke to a woman behind the desk and showed her a photo of a telegram my mum received when she was in Phoenix. It was amazing how loud the crickets were as she stared at this screen trying to look and sound interested.

Walking around the museum made me giggle as I had a flashback to when I was in the throes of my acting career at school. I was in a play which was set in the Wild West. I played a cowboy who was driving a Wells Fargo carriage, and I was opening the whole play. I had a big responsibility. Make up on, costume straight, the pressure was on. Boy did I feel it – I flopped! I forgot my lines… The silence was deafening, and I hear this whisper coming from stage right. It was the director telling me my line. I did not hear what he said so I turned to him and said in a loud whisper, "What?" Everyone laughed but I was just mortified – I think that was the day my acting career ended – very sad, the world has certainly missed out! Until now...

I managed to kill an hour or so, after which I found myself wandering around thinking where next until I found another museum, which showed the history of the Phoenix police. Again, very fascinating and another half an hour floated away. I spoke to the boy behind the counter who was in fact a historian. We chatted about the fact that Phoenix lacked much history and he said that they regretted tearing down a lot of the older buildings and not preserving history.

I went to get some lunch, and then realised that I had not gone to where I had wanted. So, I set off to find some of the places mum had mentioned or had memorabilia of in her scrap book. I went on to find Bill Johnson's Big Apple, The Flame restaurant, and her apartment on North and 4th Avenue, but sadly nothing was there.

I headed home and disappointingly, there was no being serenaded this time on the tram, but instead a very handsome guy told me that I was too pretty to stand up and offered me the seat next to him, on which sat his bag. I was very flattered but thought there must be something wrong with his eyesight. I checked that he was not talking to someone else before sitting. We had an interesting chat about the impending art walk, which happens every month on a Friday night. I really wished I could go but I would have moved on by then.

I did the Downtown LA art walk back in January and loved it. All these unknown artists display their work and the galleries open their doors. A whole community comes together plus those who are there for the art, spirit, a good night out, and the food... Whatever the reason! It is a great atmosphere and I would highly recommend it if you can go to one. I love art, but even if you are not into it, I would still recommend it. We said our goodbyes and he went one way, and I went the other...

November 1958

We decided to take the opportunity of seeing a little of Mexico as we never reached Mexico City. Our next lift was going to Phoenix, Arizona. Cotton picking was suggested, and we thought we would go for a week to give it a try. As our finances were a little low, we agreed. As it turned out we never did pick cotton as the first morning we missed the bus at 6.00am taking the workers to the fields and by the evening we had jobs as door- to-door sellers. We got an apartment for three weeks and eventually got jobs for the winter as waitresses in a very exclusive hotel in the dessert (so ended a very memorable trip which lasted two months).

03rd October 2019

I have found myself in Scottsdale, just down the road from Phoenix. This is a postcard from mum from Scottsdale, I find it amusing that she calls it a village!

"*Dear Mummy and Daddy,*

This is the little village where we do our shopping. The whole village has been designed in the Western style. We applied for jobs at Lulu Belles but had to be 21. The waitresses wear 1920's western style costumes. On the right there are usually a collection of old cowboys in their Stetsons and boots like the ones who sit on park benches in England. Things are pretty expensive here. This is only one street, there are several others.

Love Annabella"

I dropped off my luggage at the Airbnb as it was too early to check in, so I went to explore. I stopped at this converted garage, which was now a trendy, healthy place to eat, work, hang out, sip beer or drink coffee… And ladies, come and hang out in Scottsdale! I was surrounded by some very handsome men of all ages, shapes, dress styles, and I am sure, personalities! Maybe it was something in the water or heat, but boy am I impressed! I was very distracted from my writing, but I still managed a couple of hours before I went to my Airbnb.

It was pretty dire. It had never undergone modernisation since it was built so it is something your grandmother designed, and then died in. The hosts were nice but there was a very strict rule: I was not allowed to eat in my room! So, a couple of problems there.

1. I hate rules and such petty ones. Apparently, it was because someone left a half-eaten pizza under the bed. OMG stop the press! If it had been there for months and beginning to smell like something was rotting, I get it, but it was found the next day.
2. It was so awkward eating at the dining table when the hosts were sitting watching TV in the same room on the couch – not good for the digestion as I ate and ran, fast…
3. I did have contraband in my room and then threw the evidence in an outside bin… Oops!

04th October 2019

I went into Scottsdale to explore, and it was such a cute town. It really did still look a little like the postcard, just more eateries. I honestly think that it would be so easy to open a food related business here in the US – the more sugar, the better! Gelato shops, doughnuts, burgers, hotdogs…

I went into the historical society to see if I could find out where Lulu Belle's building was and what was occupying it. I asked a lady, who looked as old as Scottsdale itself, and thought she was going to be the perfect historical muse, but no. I was not sure if it was the way I was asking or if she just had lost a few marbles along the way, but she could not answer the question. She just kept going on about the Sugar Bowl. After the fourth attempt of trying to put it another way, without having to ask in French, I gave up. I showed the postcard from mum which showed Lulu Belle's, but still no clue – you guessed it – the Sugar Bowl came up again. Both the ladies were very helpful to their capabilities and confinements of just letting us know about the building it was in (an old schoolhouse). It was interesting though, seeing all the historic memorabilia, images and the story of how Scottsdale began.

I found a couple of other buildings which were there when mum came. They were brimming with cuteness. A small church and a blacksmith, then I stumbled on the opening of a boutique with different pop up stalls, so of course I had to investigate, especially when it said, 'Free drinks and nibbles'. The first table was the best – the wine table… I gratefully accepted a glass of Rosé and it was very good – the best wine I had tasted in the US so far! Was that because it was free? There were some really nice people who I chatted to and stalls selling things. Oh, had I not been broke, overweight with my luggage, and technically homeless, I would have purchased some bits and pieces, but instead I walked away with a warm, fuzzy feeling... Oh right, that was the wine!

I went to grab something to eat across from the Sugar Bowl. When I finished, I went over there wondering if that was where Lulu Belle's used to be. But no, that actually opened when mum and the girls were there back in 1958! How cool is that?

Back to my jail cell, but not for long. I decided to go shopping to Walmart – I had never been to one before, but of course they are famous! Wow... Is all I can say – I got lost in it. It was huge. It also seemed to be a crèche for parents to allow their children to let off some energy. The noise of the screaming children was deafening and fucking annoying and you had to be careful of these small beings suddenly appearing and missing your trolley by inches. But hey... Another tick off my bucket list.

06th October 2019

One of my places to visit in Phoenix, Arizona was the Camelback Inn. This is where mum and the girls worked for a few months when they ran out of money. They tried their hands at selling portraits for a photographic studio but failed dismally. They thought about Lulu Belle's too, but were not old enough. So, it was the Camelback Inn... I was excited to go as Mum had a whole scrapbook of photos and memorabilia, and I felt as if I had worked there too because of the amount of times I had looked through the stuff.

As you know, my whole journey has been about budgeting and part of that is taking public transport when I can. Sometimes it has been impossible but when I can, I do and the smaller the town or city, the more interesting it gets! People tell me to get Uber as that is cheap and easy, but when you are on the type of budget, I am on then that is still too expensive! Bus it is then – I checked it out and off I trotted to the Camelback Inn. To be honest the bus journey went fairly easily.

I was lucky as most of the time the buses only run every 30 minutes and I usually managed to just miss them, but not this time. I arrived at the stop and voila… There it was! 40 minutes later I arrived at the Camelback Inn. Okay, a quick side note here, I am not a writer. Never in my wildest dream did I think that I would be writing this book, but it has kind of taken over my life. Because of that, I go through insurmountable fear.

My 'monkey mind or ego or sense', whatever you call it, often asks me screams at me, "What are you doing? No one is going to be interested in what you have to say. You are single, broke, fluffing around the world, avoiding life and settling down… Getting a JOB!".

When I am feeling this fear, I ask mum for a sign that I am doing the right thing. The night before I went to the Camelback Inn, I could not sleep. I was worrying about money, my trip, the book, my life – I think you get it. Finally, I asked mum for a sign. Walking up this long, sweeping driveway of the Camelback Inn, I took in the beauty. Set just under Camelback Mountain, the landscape was breath-taking. I arrived at the lobby entrance and took photos. I appreciated the opulence of the five-star resort. To the side a green umbrella caught my eye, and I burst into tears and laughed at the same time; it was a Starbucks umbrella and I realised that was the sign from mum to keep going.

Another side note – when I turned thirty, I found myself living at home again. I was newly divorced, licking my wounds, and I wanted to go to New York. So, myself, mum and Jules, one of my brothers, went. We took one of those tourist buses and mum would laugh at the fact that the guide kept pointing out at each street corner where there was a Starbucks. So, every time she saw a Starbucks she would say in her really bad American accent, "And there's another Starbucks."

So, when I saw 'another Starbucks' at the resort where she worked 61 years ago, the irony was not lost. Snot coming out my nose, trying to wipe away my tears on the sly, I walked through the lobby of this very plush, beautiful resort. I, of course, bought a Starbucks where I cried again as I saw the prices. I took my coffee and went to sit in the gardens and ponder. My mission was to talk to people and even see if I could see an old employment record or something. After I gathered my thoughts, I went for a wander around when someone asked if I needed help. I went over to him and asked if he knew where a photograph I had from mum's scrapbook, was taken. We got talking and he told me that his wife was born at the hotel back in 1960, but that means that her parents worked there at the time mum and the girls did. He told me some stories and I showed him a few more photographs. He was very interested. However, he could not recall where the archway was in the photo, so we both assumed that it has gone. I thanked him and he went back to work.

I walked around more and took in the beauty of the surroundings and what they had placed in the grounds. It was like a scene straight out of a Disney movie. There was a hummingbird just in front of me getting nectar from purple flowers (it was truly magical as I had never seen a hummingbird so close). The sky was so blue, it looked like it has just been painted. The buildings blended perfectly into the mountains, and I almost thought that there should have been someone singing about the beauty of life running in the background. I could see why people would either visit or work there. I could have spent a lot longer taking it all in, but I had to go.

Off I trotted to get the bus back. Walking for 20 minutes in the searing, desert heat, I came to the bus stop where they were doing road works. They had closed off the road that I needed to use to get back… I was hot, hungry and thirsty, so I decided that my only option was to go to a resort hotel, which I had just passed, to grab some lunch and order an Uber. Again, I literally found myself in paradise. It was gorgeous! I was sure Snow White was lurking in the perfectly green bushes, waiting to burst out with her birds in tow. I smiled to myself and after a delicious lunch, I was back at the Airbnb to pack for my trip the following day.

After packing, I sat and thought about the day and the Camelback Inn, and something that Gerrie had said. If they hadn't have had to they would never have left the Camelback Inn and Arizona. The photos that I have looked at so many times are of endless parties, smiles, laughter, friendships being formed and cemented, along with bonding with locals and other workers. Also, life as an employee has been historized in the pages of mum's scrapbooks which includes an invitation by the owners, 'The Stewarts' for the staff Christmas dinner, menus from her time there, and even the leaflet which shows the rates at the time.

"*Dear Mummy and Daddy,*

This is where we went swimming. It is a lovely place (Emerald Pools). There is now a diving board at the near end and there is a juke box and an ice cream machine. I'm writing this in the bus.

How I'm going to miss Arizona. Everything is white outside. Love Annabella"

It certainly enriched the experience of my trip, and it was a privilege to be a part of history in a very small way.

        Goodbye Arizona… Hello Nevada.

Viva Las Vegas

08th October 2019

Sitting on the bus, which was certainly not as comfy and as new as the first one, but it was getting me where I need to go. Six and a half hours to go through the desert, some of the scenery took my breath away.

It looked like there was a blaze of fire simmering behind the mountains as the last of the sun went down. Darkness enveloped us until there was a faint glow of lights behind another set of mountains in the distance, which was a small town called Las Vegas! We passed Hoover Dam, and if you blinked you would have missed it…That is exactly what I did! I caught the tail end of lights. Very disappointing.

October 18th 1958

We took a bus to the outskirts and then started hitching to Las Vegas. We once again took sleeping bags and another bag. This time I rolled up some clothes in my sleeping bag and carried food in my bucket bag. Our first two lifts were short ones. At about 11.30am *we sat by the wayside and had lunch. Then we got a lift from a Mexican. We stopped at a fruit stall and bought about $1.00 worth of fruit. The Mexican bought us all root beer which none of us could bear. I walked behind and threw mine away. It was so obvious that the other two burst out laughing when I returned. I hope he didn't realise!*

He took us about 30 miles beyond San Bernardino and left us by a gas station. A car which had been getting gas stopped and two men laughingly asked us if we wanted a lift. We said yes rather doubtfully. They then asked us how old we were. At first, I wasn't going to say but apparently it is a rule that people can't take minors over a state line. However, they took us all the same. They were both teases (both called Bill) so we soon joined in with the spirit of things. One said he was called Sweet William and he called the other Jughead or Bird Brain, just so we could distinguish between them. We joked with them all the way to Vegas where we arrived at about 6.00pm. They bought us a good meal on the way. Our next port of call was Hoover Dam then the Grand Canyon.

Our next lift was an elderly married Mormon couple. The husband bought us an orange juice which we didn't really want. Then we got a lift from two boys going to see the dam. Hoover Dam was originally called Boulder Dam, but when Hoover was president the name of the dam was changed to this. In nearby Boulder City, we watched a half hour film on the construction of the dam; a really amazing feat. It was interesting seeing the dam after the film. The boys paid for us to go down into the dam on a conducted tour.

08th October 2019

I mentioned earlier that the universe has a funny way of synchronising, and when I was on the bus, I had the realisation that 13 years ago in the same month (October 2006), I was in Las Vegas with mum. We had a great time and upon that realisation, it was like a moment of grief engulfed me. Remembering our times with such fondness but also with enormous sadness because I cannot tell her of my time now. We did go to the Hoover Dam and of course, she told me of her time visiting 50 years before. I arrived at the bus stop and had a 15-minute walk to the hotel. I took my life and my luggage into my hands, scurrying through the deserted streets but managed to get there okay.

Phew… I got to my room and, I thought I had stepped into 'The Shining'. I know I am in the poor man's quarter but this place had not been updated since it was built back in the '20s. I told myself that it was okay and that it was all part of my experience, but then I went to check the bathroom and I saw blood (or what looked like it) in the bath – bloody hell. This really is 'The Shining'! Maybe the last person did not pay the bill! So, I went down to the desk and asked to move rooms. They were very nice about it and 'upgraded' me to a bigger room, but still with dodgy décor. What was very charming about the hotel was that it was 'authentic'. The black ring around the bath certainly added to the authenticity! It had not been upgraded too much, so it was not shiny and new, which is quite refreshing. The reason why I chose this hotel was because it was one of the places mum had visited.

The bright lights and buzzing atmosphere did not disappoint, and it was right on my doorstep. I was located downtown, which I had not been to before and it was great. As I arrived quite late, I took a wander out through a gambling mecca of blackjack, keno, poker, roulette tables, and of course slot machines. Outside, I was met by a blur of lights, loud music, boobs, arse, various characters, as well as people from all walks of life begging for money. It is called the 'Freemont Experience' and it was a covered road which put on a light display on the roof. Now and again people were flung on a zip wire above our heads. I could only cope with an hour of this excitement, so I retired to bed.

October 18th 1958

We looked around for a motel. We eventually got one which had adjoining rooms and a communal bathroom. We weren't very happy about it. We thoroughly tested the locks on both sides of each door in front of the men in case they had any ideas. We paid $5.00 amongst us. They went off for an hour whilst we changed then they took us to the Horseshoe Club for dinner. We weren't very hungry, so we didn't eat too much.

After that they took us on to the famous strip. It's certainly quite a sight. Flicking lights of gambling houses on both sides of the road right down the road and crowds everywhere. Las Vegas is a 24-hour, seven day a week town. Nothing ever closes. Also being a Saturday night, it was especially busy. Sweet William showed us around a little, gave us $1.00 each to spend, then left us. We limited ourselves to 50c each on gambling. We wandered in and out of every gambling place. We were thrown out of one but managed to pass in all the others by indignantly asserting that we were 21. I stuck to the nickel machines and when my 50c was gone, I continued by using nickels and dimes I found which people had carelessly left. Trust me!

We watched two different cabarets which were interesting. At 1.00 we had had enough so we waited outside the Golden Nugget for one of the Bills. Inside the Golden Nugget was $1,000,000 in notes on view. What a sight! We finally met up with both the Bills, who took us onto the Silver Slipper night cl u b where t he y had coupons for free drinks. We sat in a dark corner and had sherry and martinis. There was a very good trio entertaining. Halfway through Martha Raye came in and tried her luck for about five minutes, causing quite a stir. We eventually got into bed at about 5.00am after a very enjoyable evening in fabulous Las Vegas. We had a little trouble in getting rid of the Bills, but got the door safely locked in the end.

09th October 2019

I had some planning to do of where next on the journey, so I took my laptop and sat in the restaurant that does a buffet. Before that, I had a meeting with a published author who I thought would be good to get some tips on what to do next. I know I repeat myself but a year ago, I never thought I would be on this journey or writing a book.

I knew I wanted to write, and my business coaches were telling me to write a self-help book. That filled me with dread, and I was adamant I did not want to put out another self-help book into the market. I wanted to inspire people in a different way and amazingly through my mum's and my story – here I am! So, any tips from people in the know is gratefully received.

We met in this breakfast place, which I think is liked by the locals as it is off the tourist track. I just had a coffee which was pretty awful, strong and burnt, and it was like a magic cup – it kept refilling! It would have been gratefully appreciated, but I really did not want to drink it although I needed the caffeine and it would have been rude not to drink it. A couple of hours later, we say our goodbyes and I was armored with a few tips.

October 19th 1958

We had to be out of our motel by 11.00am. The two Bills took us to the Pancake House for breakfast where we ate far more than we should have. I was a little surprised that they bothered with us after not cooperating the night before. They drove us to a suitable hitching place, then we said goodbye.

October 2006

Mum and I stayed at the other end of the city in The Excalibur Hotel, which is famous on the strip as it is the shape of a medieval castle. Whilst we were here, we took a day trip into the desert. The trip was conducted by a cowboy who my mum took quite a fancy to. She spent the day hanging off every word he said and flirting with him. It was quite painful to watch, but funny at the same time. He told us the history of Las Vegas, which was incredibly interesting. It was a long day though.

We played blackjack one night and both did quite well. We also took part in a banquet and watched jousting as part of a show, and to top it all off we went on a sunset helicopter picnic into the Grand Canyon. It was so special as that is where she regales tales of her travels to the Grand Canyon when she was younger.

We sat on a picnic bench watching the sunset and eating a pre-packed picnic with a few others. People were fascinated by her stories, especially the one where she and the girls found a bench to sleep under and when they woke up, they were surrounded by about 20 Native American's sitting in a semicircle, just watching them! She said they gathered up their belongings very quietly and tiptoed away. The Native American's did not move, but rather just sat watching this sight. Mum said they were not sure who was more afraid of whom – them of the girls, or the girls of them. They did not hang about to find out.

I love that story and it's an experience many people have not even come close to. To be sitting in the Grand Canyon whilst the sun was setting, watching people suck up these tales, I could not have been prouder of having her as my mum. Now to be sharing this story with the world is incredible. As with anything, the time came to an end for mum and me in Las Vegas, but it is certainly a memory I keep in my heart. How lucky am I that I got to do that with not only my mother but that I got to do it at all? Feeling those feelings, I felt quite alone so I hung out in my hotel room with a glass of wine, eating some food I had stolen from the buffet. Realising that I had no cutlery to butter a roll, I had to use ice tongs as a makeshift knife but eventually realised how sad this must have appeared. So, I went out for a bit, which cheered me up.

It is funny how when you are travelling and staying in motels or hotels, you have to be creative due to the lack of utensils. Cutting up water bottles and using the bottoms as a bowl, the tongs as a knife etc… Mum had the same experience too, which I find quite amusing.

"We ate our cornflakes out of glasses and crushed up lumps of sugar."

10th October 2019

The next day, I was determined to put aside any feelings of sadness I had and go run an errand. One of the toughest parts of being on a budget in the US is getting around. As a bus or Uber ride could eat into my food allowance, I ended up walking a lot.

So, I started my three-mile stroll to find somewhere to exchange some currency. It was not early in the morning, but for a long time I was the only person around, other than the odd homeless person that is. I could not quite believe it, considering I was in the city that never sleeps! Clearly everyone was on the strip or in the casino houses, there were plenty of cars and buses. It was a great way of seeing Las Vegas so I didn't mind.

Over an hour later, tired, thirsty and hungry, I arrived at the currency exchange place, to find it is fucking closed. Oh, the expletives that came out of me, I would have to put an 18 certificate on this book. I checked Google maps again and it definitely said it was open! So, I went in search of another one. The map took me to this gigantic mall where upon entering, looking like I had just landed from outer space, a lady tells me where I need to go which is very kind. By this time, to make things worse, I was getting a blister, so now I needed to not only find this currency exchange place, but also somewhere to get a plaster... I was getting more and more frustrated, and the pain was getting worse.

Ten minutes later, at the top of the escalator – tadah! Not only the exchange place but also a giant pharmacy dispenser (it was so cool, it was like a candy or soda dispenser! I have never seen one of those before). I thought, okay, put the past behind me and all my wishes for that moment had come true. I searched eagerly with my nose pressed against the glass for plasters... Condoms, Advil, probably morphine and antidepressants – everything BUT freaking plasters...

I walked over to the currency exchange and asked the girl about the day's rate, but it was laughable. I decided against changing any money and instead I almost burst into tears with frustration. The look of pure horror on this poor girl's face was comical. She did not know what to do and thought that it was the exchange rate that had upset me. I asked her where the nearest pharmacy was, and I told her about my blister. She took sheer pity on me and told me that she had a first aid kit, managing to find some plasters. She gave them to me; I think in the hope that I would leave so she did not have to call a psychiatrist or security. I wanted to jump over the counter and kiss her but thinking better of it, I thanked her very much, found a seat, put the plaster on and left. I was on the famous strip, and I had decided that the pain had temporarily subsided, so I went to the Excalibur Hotel.

I had completely forgotten how far it was and halfway there, I gave in and jumped on a bus. Once at the stop, memories come flooding back and a huge smile appeared on my face alongside tears in my eyes. I really do have to stop this crying like this, otherwise I am going to end this journey certified! I went inside the hotel and it had not changed. I remembered where mum and I sat and had drinks and dinner, and the table on which we gambled. I was enjoying the memories when suddenly an alarm started going off. It tells everyone not to panic, until they know the source of the alarm which made me giggle.

I did at one point think how cool it would have been to go to the same table and play some blackjack, but that was not going to happen now. I did not want to get to the point of having to panic! I left the Excalibur and jumped on a bus back to my hotel. My plan had been that night to get some going-out clothes on and hit the blackjack table, but there was a part of me thinking that maybe I shouldn't as I had not had success with money-related situations that day. Did I listen to that? Hell no! I hit the blackjack table, and it took me all of ten minutes to lose my $25! Note to self… Listen to your gut instinct! Ah well, it added to my adventures. I soaked up some of the atmosphere, got bored and went off to bed.

11th October 2019

My bus did not leave until 1.30am, so I planned to hang out all day. I thought a good plan would be to go and sit in a buffet place with my laptop. It was the cheapest place I could find, and the food was the cheapest to match. I headed to the food area to start off with cheese, only to discover processed cheese slices. I think the only cheese in them was on the actual packet where it said 'cheese'. I picked up what looked like a barbeque spare rib, but I am sure it was not supposed to bounce when I accidentally dropped it! I also tried having a mouthful of the mashed potato, which I had to gulp down with half a litre of water. So, I am guessing it came from a packet and there was not a potato in sight.

I was sitting there happily, when this lady came over to me and told me that I had sat there far too long. They have a 90-minute policy, and I had exceeded that over an hour ago, so I was asked to finish up and leave! So, leave I did… It was ridiculous as nowhere was this mentioned and it was not busy enough to need the table. I was not gorging myself… But rules are rules and I indignantly walked out, mumbling under my breath with what dignity I had left!

I thought I was being really smart when I booked the overnight bus as I would not have to pay a night's hotel and I would be saving. Well now, that was not the case – I spent so much money on sitting somewhere, either getting coffee or food so I could while away the hours waiting. I was also so tired, and the brash loudness of Las Vegas' excitement soon wore off. I sat watching people partying and was glad I was not going to be them the next morning. I have found that the older I get, the worse my hangovers are, but of course I never learn!

At 01.00 am I got to the Greyhound bus station, America's oldest and probably most known bus service and I have never seen so many characters trying to escape the big city. Some had obviously been partying too much, others were trying to get somewhere as cheaply as possible. Young, old, and all genders, nationalities and economic situations. I noticed this one guy who could not stand still, buzzing with excitement. He looked unkempt but was quite well spoken. I watched him while he chatted to people, but they seem to shun him, so I started talking to him. It turned out he was going home after two years living on the streets in Las Vegas. His mum had managed to save up enough money to buy him a bus ticket. He told me his roommate up and left after introducing him to drugs and he found himself being evicted and homeless. He admitted that the drugs and drink helped him cope but he decided three months prior to kick his drugs.

Have you ever felt a connection with someone even though you have just met? I do not mean romantically, but rather I felt incredibly proud of him. I did not know him from Adam, and I thought it was a bit weird for me to tell him, so I told him he was amazing. He did not even get help for his addiction. He just woke up one day and decided to kick the habit. I told him how I could understand why people on the streets turned to drugs and alcohol to cope with the horrors that hopefully many of us do not have to face. He showed me the downside of living on the streets, explaining that he had lost one of his thumbs below the knuckle and showed me another bandaged finger that he may still lose. His thumb had to be amputated because he got a cactus needle stuck under his nail but did not have the means to get it out. It got infected and developed sepsis. He was incredibly upbeat and frank. I asked him lots of questions about his future and he was happy to answer them. I could not give him any money so instead I gave him a packet of biscuits which I was going to eat on the journey. He understood and gratefully received my offering.

Then he showed me a $10 bill he had been given and said that he was sorted for the trip home. He did, however, admit he had not showered for two weeks – I would not like to have been his seat partner. When my bus was called, I said goodbye to him and wished him good luck as he was not going to LA. I would have loved to have chatted to him more, but it was not meant to be. I will always wonder how he is doing – I hope that he got the new start he was hoping for.

October 19th 1958

When we got back up, the boys started doing a bit of reckoning and decided they would make the trip to the Grand Canyon, taking us with them. They had to be back in LA the following evening. It was wonderful for us as lifts didn't look too plentiful.

After a short while we decided we were all hungry and had a picnic of stale bread, over-ripe bananas and butter, which smelt a little off. We had long ago learnt not to make sandwiches ahead as they usually only got wasted. Later on, we stopped for a proper meal which the boys paid for. I wasn't so hungry by then which was a shame. I had boysenberry pie. It has now taken the place of hot mince in my choice.

We drove steadily on at a speed not exceeding 45 as it was rather an old car. We told jokes and stories and sang. I was sitting in the back seat with Dick who began to get a bit passionate, but I soon put a stop to it! We stopped for the night in a trailer camp. We parked by a picnic bench. The two boys slept in the car. We had our sleeping bags, so we slept out. Janet and Gerrie on top of the picnic bench and me underneath. I was rather afraid a snake would crawl into my sleeping bag during the night! It turned out to be freezing cold and lumpy and none of us slept too well. Both Janet and Gerrie joined me under the bench during the night. We certainly choose some funny places to sleep!

October 20th 1958

We woke up at 5.00am just as it was beginning to get light. I had quite a struggle getting out from under the bench! We all felt pretty scruffy, having slept in our clothes. The camps provide rest rooms so we had a wash and brush up as best we could. When we were in there several Indian Squaws in Indian costumes came in. We thought we were seeing things at first! We then discovered that we were surround by truck loads of Indians. I don't think we would have slept so well the night before if we had known! The boys built a fire which we all hugged to try to warm up. We sat on logs with our sleeping bags draped round looking very much like Indians ourselves! The boys took the car in search of some food whilst we kept the fire going.

They were gone such a long time that we began to think they had got tired of us. About an hour later they returned empty handed as the store didn't open 'til 9.00am. We packed up and set off for the Canyon. My first glimpse of it was breath taking. It really is one of the seven wonders of the world and is quite breath taking. We drove around the south rim of it until we came to the Hermits Cave (known as Hermits Rest), an unusual stone structure in the shape of a dome. It was an enormous stone fireplace where you could sit on skins drinking coffee or hot chocolate. You could also buy souvenirs there.

We had an interesting talk with an arty couple about New Orleans and S. America. They suggested we might try getting a boat from Veracruz and going to N.O. That way, we could either hitch a ride on a private boat or work our way. We left the cave at about 9.45am and after driving a little way around the rim we set off back to LA. We drove steadily 'till about 3.00pm. We were getting pretty hungry as we had only had a hot chocolate, so the first time they stopped we ordered three grilled cheese sandwiches and boysenberry pie and took them out with us to eat them on the way. We had a long discussion on families and religion right until we got back to our hotel.

This is where mum's diary ends. She gets too busy to write every day.

How Come My Arse is Growing at the Same Speed My Bank Account is Shrinking?

12th October 2019

The bus trip was pretty awful and there was not enough room. We had a wannabe matron as a bus driver who did not let us have our phones or laptops on 'because of the glare'. Sleeping was the only activity allowed as it was overnight, but I was unable to engage and was awake for most of the journey. I did, however, manage to get to my destination, which was Union Station in LA in time to get a train to San Clemente in Orange County.

En route we stopped briefly in San Bernardino, which is where mum and the girls spent a lovely night hosted by a lift. I got shouted at by the driver and the matron as I wanted to take a quick photo whilst everyone else was smoking, and I was not allowed to go to a spot where the best picture would have been taken. I was not a happy camper as this was around 5.00am, I had had little sleep, and I thought they were just plain rude. I got one photo but not the best. San Bernardino – tick!

October 10th 1958

Off again. We walked down to the bus depot and caught a bus to an outlying town. We had a coffee and a little rest there. We started to hitch again. Our first lift was with a sailor and his mother. They took us on to the highway. There, we were picked up by Paul, a boy who acted and spoke rather like Jimmy Stewart.

He was on his way to San Bernardino. At about 3 o'clock he bought us cheeseburgers, pie and coffee. He was a bit like an overgrown schoolboy but quite nice. We stopped again for supper later on. He gave us $1.00 to share between us. He drove steadily on until he arrived at his sister's house at 12.30. We crept around the house looking for a place to sleep but finally decided to sleep in the car. Janet slept on the front seat in a sleeping bag, Gerrie on the back seat, and I slept on the floor at the back with two sleeping bags under me. It was murder! Onthe journey we passed through large olive groves and vineyards.

October 11th 1958

I woke up about 8.00am with my back feeling as though it was in half, although considering my position, I had slept pretty well. A face peeped through the window at us and said, "I don't know who looks worse, you or me!" It was Paul's sister. She must have got rather a shock! We did our hair in the car then wandered into the lounge. Paul introduced us to Lea, his sister; Dick, her husband; and Bill and Marylea, their small kids. They invited us for breakfast and clean-up, which we gratefully accepted. We felt a bit awful sitting around in the lounge as though waiting to be asked. We had pancakes and eggs for breakfast. The pancakes were lovely thick ones cooked on a skillet on the table served with maple syrup. We also had orange juice and coffee and cinnamon toast, a typical American breakfast. Afterwards Lea asked us if we would like to stay another night, so we jumped at the idea! First, we began on all our washing. Lea did the whole lot for us in her washing machine. She was really wonderful and we had collected a fair amount by then. We hung everything out in the garden to dry in the sun. Whilst our washing was being done, we had baths then changed into bathing costumes, then spent a couple of hours sunbathing on the lawn. Their house was at the end of a road which ended in sand hills. It was a very peaceful place.

At about 4 o'clock Dick took us for a run in the car to see the orange groves. We ran through them for miles. Unfortunately, the oranges weren't ripe, and it was very smoggy, but it was good seeing California oranges growing. We passed some trailers on sale, so I had never seen inside one, we went to see some. The owner was very helpful and showed us four. One of them was 50 ft long and had a bar in it.

They are fantastic. When we returned Dick started a barbeque in the garden and cooked steak rolled on shelves, it smelt gorgeous! Lea cooked corn, strawberry and apple puree, beets, roast potatoes and pumpkin pie. We couldn't move after. We had a glass of Thunderbird wine which was also delicious. It also made us pretty light-headed!! Afterwards we washed up while Lea did our ironing. She really was terrific to us. We sorted out our haversacks and did some mending. We bedded down for the night in the lounge. Janet and Gerrie slept on the floor in sleeping bags and I slept on the couch in my bag. I had the honoured position because I had slept on the car floor the night before. So ends a really enjoyable day.

October 12th 1958

Dick woke us at 6.45am so that we could go to church with him at 7.30am. It was a short communion service in the Episcopal Church (Anglican). Dick and I were the only two to take communion. We got back nicely in time for a bacon and egg breakfast. After that Lea took Billy off to church. We packed our haversacks then sat in the lounge talking to Paul and Dick. Poor Marylea had a slight paralysis in her legs and although she is two, she cannot yet walk. She also has one cross eye. It seems such a shame as she is a happy little soul. We were very sorry to say goodbye to her as she and the whole family were so good to us. Dick and Paul drove us out to the highway where we got a lift almost immediately.

12th October 2019

I have gone from the madness of Las Vegas to a very quaint, opulent seaside town in Orange County, California – I have landed in paradise! A few days of peace and quiet!

Due to my budget travelling, I am certainly not able to book places that are more than a one- or two-star motels, or cheap Airbnbs. However, I did mention to someone that I would love to stay in an authentic American Motel. I think the person I said it to laughed at me. So, I found myself in a two-star motel on the side of a busy road and when I walked into my room, I realised why he laughed at my idea… All I can say is be careful what you wish for! The smell hit me first; musty with the aroma that something died mixed with stale cigarette smoke. The colour of the first wall looks like something vomited on it with some cobwebs. I cannot quite believe that this is actually a paint colour! The second wall is blood red – enough said! I swear, I am not making this up! I closed one of the shutters and there was either red paint or something splattered on it… My neighbours were an interesting mix of people. Yes, I did get to hear them as the walls and floorboards didn't have soundproofing. That night was a mixture of loud sex, a girl crying, comings and goings, and kids not sleeping. Oh, I was in for a treat!

13th October 2019

Today was the usual exploratory trip around San Clemente and a walk on the beach and pier… It was surfers' paradise and something straight out of the movies or 'Baywatch'. Watching the locals of the 'OC' was fascinating. There were women who had not eaten more than an ice cube since their last birthday, with faces pulled back so far you could see their skeletal features. The men walked proudly with their wives or girlfriends, with a panic behind their eyes, knowing that if they did not have the bulk of their personality in their bank account, they would not have stood a chance. Then there were the dogs – who were pampered just as much as the kids – and polite teenagers… It was, as I say, something out of a movie.

Then, right on cue, to break the perfect spell, a fight between two men occurred. They were cursing and squaring up to each other until they were broken apart. The sun and sand had obviously got to them and not in a positive way, but hey, you get it wherever you go. I got lost walking back to my room, so I ended up going a very long way around, but it was okay. I loved seeing all the Halloween decorations. I later fall into bed exhausted but happy.

14th October 2019

I decided to go to the Mission in San Juan Capistrano, which is the birthplace of Orange County and a historical landmark. I had the option of jumping into an Uber (as it was not that expensive), which would be much more convenient and a ten minute car ride, and boy was I tempted BUT I committed to doing this journey as true to how mum and the girls would have done it. So, I started off for the bus stop instead.

There was also a train that would have taken me there, but the track only had one line, so it only goes in one direction at a time. Well, that was no good… I arrived at the bus stop and of course, I had just missed it, so I was in for a 25-minute wait. It was rather awkward as there were two police cars and a police bike talking to a 'suspect' just next to me. From what I gathered, he was being accused of stealing a bike and he was trying to talk his way out of it. It really did look like I had just stopped to watch this unfold, but hey it added some entertainment. Two buses, and an hour later, I arrived, but luckily the mission did not disappoint. It was absolutely stunning and so peaceful. I spent a few hours sucking up the history, taking photos and imagining mum and the girls wandering around it too. Not looking forward to the long bus ride home, I tried to bargain with myself about getting an Uber, but I reminded myself that I had to pay extra for the admission to the mission – that is the fun and games of being broke! So, off I trotted to the bus stop and waited… For 45 minutes. After a 30-minute ride, I got off to jump on another bus but decided that I couldn't be bothered to wait for yet another bus, so I walked home.

I arrived home and settled into my evening of catching up on some TV, but I was getting agitated by the next-door neighbours. They were going in and out of the door, literally every five minutes and letting it slam. The doors were quite heavy and seemed to shake my room walls and doors like a 5.6 magnitude earthquake. I was sure it was the kids, thinking they would go to bed soon, but then the parents started opening and slamming the door like a brothel on a good night. I was pressured to get a good night's sleep as I had to be up early in the morning for a radio interview and I hoped that this noise was not going to go on for too long. I think the last slam of the door was at 11.15pm.

I wish that was all the frustration, but no. My upstairs neighbours decided to start moving furniture around like they were setting up for a yard sale and I think they had invited the whole neighbourhood for a soiree. All I could think about was my friend laughing at me telling me, "What did you expect?"

15th October 2019

I am not one for complaining. Okay, yes, I am, I am British! So, I complained to the front office in the morning and asked for another room. The woman behind the desk told me that the family next door was checking out today, and she would speak to the upstairs people. I really did not want to pack my luggage, so I agree to wait.

Before I went to the front office, I put some jeans on, and when I put them on, they were 'snug' and not tight. I was very proud of myself, thinking that all the walking I had done was negating and beating the calories from the burgers, wine, chocolate, and fries I had been eating… Whoop whoop! I walked to Starbucks to do some writing, taking in the surroundings, and life in a surf village. There was a guy who sped past me in his Porsche convertible, sunnies on, looking like he is successful. I then chuckled to myself as I saw him park outside a launderette and getting some clothes out of the car. I thought to myself, he has spent all his money on his car with no money left for a washing machine! Oh, the irony.

I arrived at Starbucks, and there are lots of people working away on their laptops and community leaflets on the notice board. The barrister was saying hello to people he knew, and lots of different people were coming and going, all wanting their Starbucks fix. I loved it – feeling part of the community. This longing bubbled up in my stomach as that was what I missed desperately – being part of a community. Travelling, you are an outsider and not part of anything, so it can add to the loneliness, but you know you have made the community when the Starbucks barrister knows your name. I sat for a few hours, watching, writing and more watching, then headed back. When I got there, I thought that I would sit for a while and see how the noise was, realizing that the neighbours had obviously moved on. Not as much slamming of doors and walls shaking. I was glad as the room that the lady behind the desk said I could move to was in the main building, above where they clearly lived. The owners had cooked a curry and I really do not like the smell. It lingers too… Give me the musty smell of death and stale smoke over that!

16th October 2019

I managed to have a much more peaceful sleep so when I woke up, I packed, ready to move on. Whilst packing I put all my jeans on the bed, when I noticed that the jeans which were 'snug' on me yesterday were NOT my skinny jeans as I had thought.

They were to my horror, my FAT jeans! The jeans I wear which have… room! Fuck! I recoil in horror as it dawns on me what that means… My bank account was the only thing that is going down! How does it happen that my arse was growing at the same speed that my bank account was shrinking? Humph…

The weather had taken a turn with the fog rolling in like smoke, but it added to the charm of San Clemente. I was catching the surfliner train which ran from San Diego to Los Angeles mostly along the coast. It was recommended that I took it to watch the views. Well, of course, typically, I choose the only day the fog rolls in, so I couldn't see much! From what I did see, it was lovely and well worth the journey. One and a half hours later, I arrived at my destination, wishing it had taken a lot longer.

San Diego – My Paradise!

My mum and her friends spent one night in San Diego, then they hitched a ride with a plumber to get to Mexico. They reached Mexicali, Mexico for one night, where they were taken to a strip joint. Being fairly naïve and young at that time, they were quite shocked. It was under the guise of going to a 'club type bar'. That was their Mexican experience. This was not their plan – they had wanted to go for much longer and explore.

16th October 2019

Ah, San Diego… Where the traffic lights sound like birds chirping and the sunshine never ends. Oh, and where the dog parks have beautifully manicured grass! I have arrived…

I finally get to my motel, which should have only taken ten minutes to walk to from the train station, but it actually took over an hour. This was due to the pavements not being conducive to lugging over 100 lbs in two suitcases. The motel was not in the best area and there were a lot of homeless people around, so I felt that I blended in with all my worldly belongings. No one seemed to really bat an eyelid! The hotel was basic but clean. I didn't unpack but just opened my suitcases. I had stopped unpacking, as it was not worth it for a couple of days' stay. There was a part of me that really wanted to get rid of stuff so it was not so heavy and annoying, but I didn't know what I would let go of. Putting those thoughts aside, I decided to explore the area and grab some groceries. It wasn't an exciting evening, but I got into bed exhausted.

17th October 2019

I decided to do one of my most favourite things when travelling: jump on a tourist bus. However, in San Diego, it was a tourist trolley… The only downside of the tours was that they were so expensive, but this is research, right? What I tend to do is the whole tour which averages a couple of hours then I decide which stops to go back to. It cuts out a whole lot of time visiting places which are the supposed 'must see' but are not all that. This is and always has been my preference when visiting cities.

My driver was, of course, the overly annoying guide whose jokes were scripted and badly acted. The only people who laughed were the elderly or people who were embarrassed for him. It was, however, a great way to see San Diego. It was a beautiful day but a little windy on the trolley, so I was getting a free hair blow dry – probably a more overly back combed look!

We came to the Island of Coronado, which is another gorgeous, quaint seaside town. I fell in love with it and began to understand why people visit it or live there. I actually decided to jump off the trolley bus, mostly because my bladder was screaming at me! But also, I could not resist this paradise, and I ended up in this adorably cute place, which I was obviously drawn to as it is a French wine bar.

I found a table outside and settled down. I sat there watching the world go by, the token pug dog in a pushchair (why?), the yummy mummies, the older well-dressed ladies, gents and of course, the tourists. The waitress walked past me with a glass of rosé, I wanted to grab it and run or hoped that she would trip, and the contents of the glass would end up in my mouth! No such luck... THEN behind me the server was describing some wines to a group of people and I began salivating! And a wine pairing with a cheese board... Oh God help me... Be strong! It was the perfect setting for a glass of rosé. I could not have one and if I did, it would have been downhill all the way! I finished my coffee and ran before I caved in, found the trolley stop, and jumped on.

Later, I found myself sitting at the top of the Hyatt. I had gone to do some writing with a view! Okay, maybe it was because I found a voucher for 50% off a glass of wine... Enough said! The view was probably spectacular, but it was too cloudy. However, I quite happily sat there, ordered a half price glass of wine and did some writing.

The quiet hum of chatting got louder and louder as the evening wore on. Businessmen, people from a conference, and couples on date nights, all contributed to the background noise. A woman with fluffy balls on her head? (Ummm...Okay... Christmas decorations maybe?) a man trying to entertain a toddler who was not impressed. The weirdness just went on...

Suddenly, the lights were turned out so I could no longer see. I asked the waiter if this was normal, and he said, "Yes, it is time." Geez, there is mood lighting and no lighting at all! I did not even have enough light to see the bill so would they have argued if I underpaid? The experience was certainly under the five stars; far too noisy, the lighting was ridiculous, and I was pissed off... The only saving grace was my 50% wine!

18th October 2019

Upon waking, I decided to go to an all-American Diner for breakfast. There are millions of them around the country, so I thought it would have been quite good... Have you ever been so disappointed you cry? No? Okay, it is just me then.

It was packed when I got there, so I put my name down on the 'list' and waited. The woman next to me was slurring her words and talking very loudly to her partner so I guessed what kind of clientele this place generated, but I tried not to judge (the snobbiness comes out now and again still!)

I was called to a booth and sat down when the waitress asked if I wanted orange juice or coffee. I answered that I wanted coffee, knowing that these places are free refills so I could get my day's caffeine in, in one go. When the coffee arrived, I saw that there was a huge crack in the mug, so I sent it back. A new cup was plonked in front of me, then I was ignored for ages until I got the attention of a server, who was very under-friendly. I told her that I wanted the healthy breakfast and went about my business.

There was a child who would not stop screeching, which was drawing everybody's attention, including mine. The mother did not seem to be doing anything about it and it really was not pleasant. I put my earphones in to drown out this god-awful sound, which lessened the screeching but did not drown it out completely... Joy!

My breakfast arrived, but it was the wrong dish, so it was sent back. I had also ordered a side of sausage, which was delivered. These sausages looked like they had been freeze-dried, released into the wild, eaten by an animal, then reconstructed after being shitted out. They were the most pathetic things I had ever seen. Shriveled within an inch of its life, it looked like it had had been genetically modified to not look anything like or taste like a sausage. My proper breakfast arrived but with no cutlery. So, ten minutes later, after finally managing to get someone's attention, I had a knife and fork literally thrown on the table. I started eating it and it was okay but nothing I would write home about. I certainly was not getting that friendly, refill my coffee, and have a chat with the server vibe which was in all the movies and TV shows when in a diner.

I was asked if I wanted a refill of coffee, to which I jumped on and said yes. She came and plonked the bill down and I glanced at it. She had charged me for the wrong breakfast and then the sausages came to double the price! Wow, I thought… Maybe the sausages had been so modified and over-frozen or rare, that they were some secret recipe! However, I told her she had charged me incorrectly, and that I thought the sausages were under the meal deal. She explained it wasn't, so I told her I would not have ordered them at the price they were charging.

She went off with a mutter of, "I shall see what I can do." When she arrived back at my table, she told me that she would take the coffee off, but still charged me for the tendrils. This was obvious as the coffee was cheaper! I sat there a little longer and realised the offer for a refill of coffee was not coming… A little tear filled my eye and fell down my cheek. I was exhausted as I did not sleep well the night before, and I was made to feel that the fuck ups of the servers and the in hospitality was my fault.

Sometimes on my journey, I have felt that if I am in a predominantly Spanish area, that they can't be bothered with me or that I do not get the same service because I don't speak Spanish. This is all life learning and lessons to be more tolerable about things that are not in my control. So, I paid without leaving a tip and went back to my hotel, so upset and disappointed with my all-American diner experience. I felt sorry for myself for a little bit, so I watched TV and did some work. I then decided that I only had a short time in San Diego, so I better get my big girl's pants on and get out there. Go and explore! I went back to the Old Town, with the knowledge that this was where mum must have gone as there was a lot of architecture, dating back to the 16th century and part of Old San Diego. It was great to see. I went into a museum which gave the history of the cowboy and transportation. It was all very enchanting. San Diego, as many of you know – but for those of you who do not know – has a very Spanish feel and Mexican history, as it sits virtually on the border of Mexico.

I was there just before their festival Día de Meuertos, which is Day of the Dead. During this time. The colourful skeletons for Día de they celebrate the lives of instead of people mourning their loss. There were colourful skeletons, skulls, shrines and alters to remember those who have died. It was fascinating to see, and it was great to be a part of it. I walked around amongst oversized skeletons wearing prom dresses and suits as if they were off to get wed. The colours were vibrant, and the skulls and skeletons were certainly not scary like in a horror movie.

Tired and hot I headed back to my hotel to do some research and to think of where I was going next. I decided to stay in San Diego for the weekend as I had not seen much of it at all and I was quite smitten by it. That evening I went to the grocery store and pharmacy, not knowing that the trip would haunt me…

19th October 2019

Checking out of the one hotel into another, I left the Old Town area and headed for Little Italy. Before I did that, I put some ear drops in my ear, which I bought from the pharmacy the night before and boy was that the wrong decision.

A very quick backstory and no details to gross you out, but I sometimes need my ears syringed… Enough said, you get it surely? I felt like I was getting to that point of needing to do it again, but I was trying to hold off until I left the US. So, at the pharmacy the night before, I explained the situation to the girl behind the counter and she recommended these drops. I tell her that drops tend not to work as they just sit there and give me swimmers ear, but she reassured me it was the best way to go. Fast forward to me sitting on the bed and putting the drops in…I put them in while praying that she was right and my ears would clear, but of course, they didn't. Instead, they clogged up and I couldn't hear a bloody thing. The irony of this was that for most of my recent travels, I had not been out at night, but that night I had signed up for a pre-Halloween karaoke party! But… I was now fucking deaf! How was I going to go along to this event and make a good impression if I couldn't hear anything? I was going on my own and didn't know anyone else, so I did not have a translator! Oh, dear Lord…

I arrived at my new hotel and dropped off my luggage. The hotel was so cute. It was a restored building from 1920, and although some of the fixtures were probably still from that era, it was cosy, warm and right next to a main road! Oh, and the airplanes were literally landing in the garden! I loved that as I really enjoy watching airplanes. Aside from that it was so much better than what I had come from, so I was happy. I went off to do a little exploring. There was a farmers' market a few yards away, so I joined the locals and wandered around, trying samples of food and healthy drinks in the sunshine. After a while, I realised that I could no longer walk around with my ear blocked and hurting, so I searched for a walk-in emergency clinic to get them syringed. Most of the afternoon was taken up with this task.

I arrived at this clinic and they quoted me $500 for the procedure! Holy shit! After picking myself off the floor, I declined but she very kindly gave me a list of cheaper alternatives. I was contemplating what to do but started to head to my hotel to grab a shower then decide if I still wanted to go out.

I was, as usual, getting lost and I walked past this new holistic pharmacy. Liking the interior, I went in and explained the situation to the pharmacist just in case she could help me. She could not do the syringing but suggested an alternative. It sounded dubious but at that point I was willing to try anything rather than spending far too much money and time on the issue... I got back to my hotel and with a prayer and a wish I put more drops in... Holy moly it worked! I had 95% of my hearing back... Afterwards, I was still in two minds as to whether I should go out. Was this all a sign that I should not go? But as I had bought my costume, I felt that I couldn't waste the money and decided to go. I wore a headdress and put fake blood on my face, thinking to myself that I looked good enough. So, I jumped into an Uber as I did not think that I could go on public transport looking like that. I was dropped off outside this dingy bar, but I crossed my fingers and walked in. I was met by the organiser who, thank goodness, was dressed up too, as a mermaid. She was lovely and welcoming, which made me relax a little. She asked a little about me then introduced me to others. Luckily, everyone else was dressed up in our party (I feared that I was going to be the only one) but no one was dressed in the horror theme – they seemed to be more at a costume party. There was a ladybird, a referee, a lightning bolt, mermaid, geisha, and a man in a white latex suit with foam muscles. He had made the costume himself and identified himself as a Marvel character. The most exciting part of the evening was the initial walk in.

Unfortunately, the evening took a nosedive into boredomville, despite my attempts of chatting to people, so I left early. It is always hit and miss at these meetups. I have done a few in my travels, so I take them with a pinch of salt.

20th October 2019

I woke up and my ear felt okay. Not great, but I put in drops and it seemed to be livable. I decided to go and see more of San Diego, so I went down to the port and the seaport village. It was a blazingly sunny day and I was loving it, but in the back of my mind, I had not yet sorted out where I was staying for the next few days, so that had to be my main focus for today. My whole body and spirit were crying out for me to stay in San Diego, but my mind said that I must continue my journey and go to LA, so I could get to Catalina Island. I then understood why mum loved it here in San Diego so much!

Meltdown

21st October 2019

Today was not a good day. I was in a funk and I could feel it in my bones. I woke up to find my ear was blocked. Shit… I really didn't want to go to a doctor as I could ill afford it, so I put one set of drops in and waited and waited… It opened up slightly and I could hear a little more than I could before. So, I tried the other drops as I thought that it couldn't get any worse! That didn't help, so I gave up and prayed to the hearing gods that they could fix my ears in the next few days.

I packed AGAIN as I was going back to LA for a few days. My enthusiasm for packing was zero to none. Every time I stopped somewhere, I promised myself that I would organise my suitcases better so that I had to open one suitcase only, unless I needed my 'speciality' clothing. I blindly tried to pack for all occasions, including slightly colder fall days. I obviously didn't need those, YET! so they were going into my 'speciality' clothing space. Because I always ended up packing at the last moment, I didn't have any organisational time, clothes and shoes were flung in, hoping that the suitcase elves and fairies – whilst on the bus – would fold them neatly and iron them by the time I arrived at my next destination…

I managed to close the suitcases and refrained from throwing them down the stairs. I checked out and began my krypton factor walk through the streets of San Diego with my luggage, trying not to squash the little dogs, avoid people's toes or tripping myself up. As I was not in the best of moods, I really wouldn't have cared less if I did get any of them. I arrive at the area from where I was supposed to pick up the bus, but there was no sign, or any indication whatsoever, of where I needed to be. So, I began panicking and it was not easy to panic with over 100 lbs of luggage. Of course, there was no one to ask… I was running around, getting hotter and sweatier. I tried to find a way to contact the bus company, tapping on my mobile screen with the expectation that it knew I was in a panic and that it should cooperate at the speed I needed it to, but on the fucking app it just said 'No internet'. The bus was due any minute and I was just about to burst into frustrated tears when I saw this sea of green and orange coming towards me. Yay, the bus!

So, I started running as fast as I could as it went around a roundabout and kept driving in the other direction! I was running after this fucking bus, with my luggage, hoping that I had not missed it. When I am running, I am certainly no Baywatch beauty; I had a pained look on my face, the fat on my stomach was jogging up and down – not in unison with me, my sunglasses were falling down, my hair was sticking to my sweaty face, and I was trying not to drop my suitcases or bags!

With a stroke of luck, it stopped around the corner. I kept running until I reached it, nearly ploughing into a family, where the driver asked for my name. I think I was having a near death experience, but I managed to whisper my name to him. He nodded and took one of my suitcases, putting it in the bus casually. No big deal, just another day, manana, manana, hakuna matata, nothing to see here folks... Not noticing what I have just been through, even though I look constipated but hey, I made it! I always let people take the smaller suitcase as I am worried if anyone were to lift my bigger suitcase, they would get a hernia. I loaded the other one myself and boarded the bus. I sat down and I am not sure what happened next, but it felt like a bug jumped down my throat and started strangling me. I started having a coughing fit. I drank water, tried to clear my throat and tried not breathing, but nothing worked... Oh joy... I couldn't seem to catch a break. I even moved seats to stop the coughing (there was logic somewhere in that!)

We drove to the next stop for more people to board. All sorts of people were boarding, including couples, young backpackers, students, and the purple haired, pierced girl. It is a funny phenomenon that it seems people with larger than normal noses are travelling today!

I finally stopped coughing after 20 minutes and sat back to enjoy the rest of the ride. The trip went smoothly so I tried to laugh at what had gone wrong, but with the fear of what else could go wrong. I was still not in a great mood, and maybe I knew something was not quite right. We arrived at Union station in LA where I disembarked and unloaded my cargo, heading off towards Long Beach. Just over another hour consisting of a metro and bus ride later, I arrived. I started on my 29- minute walk through the streets, and it looked like I had either arrived in post-apocalyptic America or a third world area. There was dog shit everywhere, nappies and trash strewn around the gardens, and the area was very, very rundown. The people did not seem threatening, but I was praying that where I was staying would be okay (Snobbiness meter on overdrive!)

I arrived and looked up at this building, which on first impressions should have been knocked down years ago. I have always learnt not to judge, as the inside may be a palace. I had to climb two flights of stairs with my luggage, which was not an easy task, but I managed. I stopped to catch my breath at the top and noticed the dead flies, dirt and broken window on the landing. Still puffing and panting, I opened the door to my palace, but I have stepped into a hell hole or another dimension.

The owner was there tidying, and he was very welcoming. I was shown my room and how everything worked. When he was finished talking, I closed my bedroom door and consoled myself that is was only going to be for five nights. My room was okay, small, hot but clean. I had not, at that stage, looked around the rest of the place yet… I chatted a little more to the owner, a young professional who seemed clean, sociable, knowledgeable and kind. He told me about this job, where he was from, and recommended a burger place. He was talking a little too much, so I made my excuses, gathered my things and headed out to do some work and grab something to eat. I ran the gauntlet through the neighbourhood. The houses were very run down, there was trash in the gardens, broken windows, and fences, etc. But the kids were squealing with delight playing with each other, and the dogs, standing guard outside their properties. I walked past the museum of Latin American Art and it reminded me of my old bosses who collected Contemporary Latin American Art and I thought I would like to go in at another time.

There were still a few people around on the streets and the light was beginning to fade. I found this really cute place and settled down to write. I ordered some amazing, healthy food; a beet salad and roasted brussel sprouts with bacon. When it arrived, my eyes lit up. I was eating the beet salad and there was a yoghurt dressing over it. When I bit into it, I realised that it was made from goat… I am not a fan of goat's cheese, yoghurt, or milk and I could taste it. It reminded me of a childhood nightmare – I HATE the taste. So, I left it but ate the other bits. Great, I thought, even my dinner is against me! I sat there for as long as I felt okay as I did not want to walk through the neighbourhood too late in the dark. I asked for the bill, mentioning the yoghurt dressing, and saying that I thought I read it was a citrus, yoghurt dressing… It turned out that they had changed the recipe but not mentioned it on the menu, so they took that off the bill, which was very nice. They say things come in threes… I arrived back at the Airbnb and just as I am opening the front door, I was hit with a major smell of marijuana. I opened the door more and there on the sofa are two people trying very hard to hide the drugs (I must mention that in the state of California, recreational use of marijuana is legal, so I am not sure why they were hiding the drugs). If they wanted to hide it from me, it was bloody obvious from the smell. I was sure they were watching porn too! We all mumbled hello to each other, and I headed to my room. I completely understand it is people's choice and lifestyle, but I have grown up seeing the effects of long-term drug use and I hate the smell of marijuana, so my choice is not to be anywhere near it. Fuck, bollocks, wank… I knew I was unable to stay.

It should have been mentioned on the listing and then I would not have gone anywhere near the place. I then unearthed the rest of what contributes to the hell that I found myself in. I was in the most disgusting, dirty frat house with a bunch of pot smokers! Oh, this day had literally topped it! I got onto Airbnb telling them I could not stay there. It was a fight, but we all agreed that it was too late, and we would sort it out in the morning.

22nd October 2019

By 11 am I had left one hell hole for another one. I booked another room and headed there to find it was a motel (I do not even think it had a star rating it was so bad). It was definitely the worst accommodation I have ever stayed in. I would not have put my worst enemy there. Airbnb had agreed to refund my money from the marijuana house so that was good! At this point, I felt completely overwhelmed, exhausted, ill (my ear was completely blocked and painful, so I needed to go find a clinic to get it sorted), kicked emotionally and spiritually. I started to wonder again if the journey was worth all the shit I was experiencing. My fear of lack of money was enormous and all- encompassing.

This, having to spend hours on end scrolling through the internet for cheap accommodation, and then ending up in these places – which to be honest should be condemned – and to top it all, it didn't have working internet. The room was dark, dirty, unkempt, and the only thing it would have been good for, was for a scene in a horror movie. There was a part of me that felt that I deserved this as I had lost all my money a while back and I was wanting to write this book instead of getting a job. I felt like I had made my bed, so I was going to have to lie in it… I had no time to stop and think as I needed to get to the doctor. My mood was still in the funk, and I was fighting the urge to run back home... Or anywhere else, especially back to San Diego but, I don't have a home, so I felt very lost and alone.

The clinic was an hour's bus ride away at a place which turned out to be the most adorable seaside town in Orange County. It was unbelievably quaint. I was literally running on empty with no energy or capacity to think, so I just walked around the town as I was early for my clinic appointment.

I was soaking up the beauty and loving it, while thinking about my situation. The sun was beating down and the streets were clean. The boutiques, organic coffee shops, and the friendly people. I decided to walk along the pier when I suddenly started to hear this conversation from these two guys behind me. It was an older man, I would estimate in his late 60s (though, I am terrible at ages!) with his friend, who was an Asian American in his 30s. They were chatting about love and life, and the older man was asking the younger one for his advice. The younger man was giving him simple advice but with kindness and no judgement. This got me thinking about my situation again and how I would feel in five years' time if I gave up on my destiny of writing this book. I knew it was not what I wanted, I wanted to finish this journey and this story. I had to dig deep for that self-belief, face the fear straight in the face and use buckets of resilience to get through this. I was on this path to inspire you, the readers, and I on me without them or I knowing. They were talking about regret and what they should do. I then thought about must go back to my 'why'... Why was I writing this book?

I arrived at the clinic and the doctor was lovely and very inspired by my book, travels and stories. It was almost a sign that I had to keep going! To make matters worse of the last 24 hours, I had to get a bus back to my motel in Long Beach, so I use Google Maps to figure out my journey – which if any of you know, it is impossible to see where the bus stops are! I spent at least 20 minutes walking around in a circle trying to find the right bus stop until I thought I had the right one. But, nope! A few stops down the line I realised that I was on the wrong bus! Going the wrong fucking way! I was sure the universe was having a laugh. I was also on a time constraint as I had a conference call in an hour, and I had forgotten my earphones... Bollocks, wankety fuck.

I finally got back to my motel and breakdown... Heartful, deep sobs. I spoke to my mentor who helped me realise that all that was happening in my life was magnified because I felt that huge lack of control. Everything that was going wrong was not in my control (money, accommodation, travelling, being ill etc.) and oh by the way, the anniversary of my mum's death was coming up in four days.

I was feeling all those feelings again when she was in the hospice and all through her illness. I felt hopeless and completely helpless – I could not take the illness, pain or impending death or shit away.

My Mum – My Hero

I think this is a great time to take a pause, grab some wine, tea, or something stronger. I want to talk a little right now about my mum and our relationship in more detail. When I was growing up, my relationship with my mum was not easy. She lost her husband when she was 36. I lost my dad when I was only four.

She had four kids and a business. There was not the support back then as there is nowadays, so the five of us fumbled through life and grief the only way we knew how. As a girl growing up, I really only knew mum in the throes of grief. She withdrew and I felt that she was not there for me emotionally.

I managed to escape the shittiness of a home life filled with grief, anger, and resentment by going to boarding school, which almost saved me. Boarding school put me into a bubble of a standard of life and that is where the snobbiness began. I ate any of my feelings, needs and voice away, so my weight was a huge issue for me physically. Mum shaped the way I felt about myself physically by her loathing the way she looked and her constant dieting. I thought that was normal. My brothers were pretty brutal too, with their words, but mum told me to ignore them, not realising the damage it was doing.

On the outside we had everything. We lived in a big house

with a swimming pool, all of us kids were at private schools, we had two holidays a year, and we made some good memories. There was lots of laughter, but there was also so much pain, which I managed to self-silence. Now and again windows of behaviour, which added to the self-loathing through shame, showed that I was deeply hurting and crying out for help, but nobody noticed. Most people only saw a girl who was helpful, kind, good, and would do anything for anyone. I never voiced how I felt, and if I did, I was told to stop being so silly. I made the decision never to trust or rely on anyone.

As a perfectionist, I set myself up to fail and reaffirm, "See, you are a fuck up." I put unrealistic expectations on others so they would fail, and I could say, "See, Sophie, people let you down, you are not worth anything better." However, I remember when I was about 18 years old, I went to mum as something was going on in my life and I wanted to tell her about it. I cannot remember the details, but she began to give me advice and I got really cross with her and told her all I wanted her to do was listen to me. I just wanted her sympathy, and a great big hug… Then wash it down with a very large glass of wine. That was the turning point of our relationship and for me as a person, as it was the first time I spoke up for what I wanted. The next time I went to her, I remember she sat there intently listening. At the end she gave me a hug, and said she was sorry about what I was going through. She then turned around to me and said, "How did I do?"

I loved her more than ever in that moment. I knew how difficult it was for her to open up too. From that day, she became my life mentor, hero, best friend, travel partner, advice giver (when asked), best hugger, and the person by whom I was inspired. I sit here today writing these words with tears in my eyes as I miss her desperately every day. I still hear her voice, feel her soft skin, see her smile and remember her cheeky spirit and child- like moments. I am so grateful for my relationship with her. Unfortunately, some of the thoughts and beliefs I have had and still have, were ingrained when I was younger, more vulnerable, and a sponge. I am still healing every day and this journey is part of that.

Mum was diagnosed with terminal cancer in March 2008. It was secondary cancer and they think she may have had it for about two years, but it never gave any symptoms, which is good as she was terrible at being ill. She was given the choice to do chemotherapy, which would prolong her life for about three months. When you are told you are dying and the prognosis is six months, then hearing you could have another three months, you jump at it.

She decided to do the chemotherapy, and I remember going with her. She sat there in the chemo chair with a huge drip in her arm laughing and joking with the nurses. She had a fantastic sense of humour; she was so warm to everyone... Not knowing that the chemo she received nearly killed her four days later. She had an angina attack, and so she said no more. She decided to put the cancer in the hands of God to say when she was due to go.

We spent the next five months doing stuff. She and I managed to squeeze in one more trip to see family. She ended up in a hospice for the last eight weeks of her life, before putting on her bejazzled wings, and leaving me, my brothers, family, friends and everyone else who knew and loved her.

Two days before she passed away, I was called at work to be told that her condition had changed. I jumped into the car and sped down to the hospice, leaving behind a ticket to a gala I had bought (That was going to be my first night out in weeks! Mum certainly was going out with a bang!) When I got to the hospice she had fallen into a coma, and we knew it was not long to her end. I spent as long as I could with her that evening and the next day too. When leaving the following day, I told her, as I did every time, "Love you very much". She woke from her coma and said, "Love you very much," and then fell back into it again. Those were the last words she ever spoke. She died the next day, waiting for us to be with her. It was very important to me that I was there when she died. My fear was that she would die alone, and luckily that did not happen.

For a long time, I felt incredible guilt and carried it with me. I felt guilty that those were the last words she spoke and in response to me. Jules, my brother who was very close to her too, was also in the room. He later told me that he told her he loved her when he left later that evening, but she did not wake up. I tried to justify my moment by saying that she probably meant to say what she did to everyone and not just to me. He was not affected as deeply as I was and told me not to worry about it. It is only now, that I own, am proud of, and treasure that last moment I had with her. I know she meant it for him and the others too… After she died, I had dreams about her and in the initial days, I would wake up and for those first few seconds everything was good, and I thought mum was still alive. Then the realisation that she was gone would engulf me. She kept dying every day, and those were the most heart-wrenching moments, alongside having the phone call asking if she was a donor. I told them that she was, but because of the chemo she had received, she could not donate her organs. But what about her eyes? Her eyes… Eyes are the gateway to the soul… It was a very painful call, but I knew what mum wanted, so I gathered every inch of strength I had left, and I said yes. They couldn't take them in the end as they, too, had been poisoned by the chemo. I think that was the hardest part to deal with as most of the days after her death, I was in a haze of organising the funeral. Mum had organised most of it whilst she was still alive. She had found a venue, the caterers, the vicar, and the church. This was all to make it easier for us in the aftermath. We stuck to her wishes on all of it but one detail. We also added our own touches which made it more personal.

My dreams have evolved over the last few years. At the beginning, they would usually be that she was alive again, but no one seemed to notice or mention or make an issue out of it, and then she would then die again, decaying slowly. I had those dreams many times… They did change and she stopped dying. I remember one of the most memorable dreams was when she hugged me in my dream. Writing this today, I can still remember it so clearly. I could feel her soft skin against my cheek, her smell, the sound of her voice, and the warmth from her hug. I had a dream last night. I mention all of this as I have not dreamt of her in a while… Last night she was back in my dream, as though it was normal. She had died but she was back again…I am not afraid of the dreams, in fact, I invite them as it can be calming. The energy around her death, our relationship, my situation now, and the lack of control is very much in my psyche. So, I was reminded to pull back and the priority now is to stop, simplify and look after me and keep telling my mum's and my story. I encourage you reading this to think about your relationship with your mum or the relationship you had with your mum, if she is no longer in your life. Even if you are a mum yourself… It can be an incredible, special bond.

THERE'S ALWAYS A HITCH

Remember that it can be taken from you suddenly…

Long Beach Part Deux

23rd October 2019

I woke up still with a little residue of funk, but I did have some red wine the night before so it could have been a little of that too. I was looking forward to the day as I was meeting a friend, Marie, whom I met the last time I was in LA. She is a powerhouse of a person who is incredibly interesting to talk to. She is one of those people who knows a lot about everything. She has done so much, gone through so much and still has a satiable appetite to learn new things.

On my way there, my journey, which was only a ten-minute walk, was interrupted by a commercial being shot on the streets. It was for a car commercial and it was amazing how much of a setup there was for a two second shot! It never ceases to amaze me how Hollywood, television, and the movies come together. I lingered watching, as I was asked to wait until the scene had finished, also secretly hoping they would ask me to be a part of it all! As the shot finished, I walked on… they clearly had not heard of my acting skills yet!

I arrived at the lunch place early so that I could use their

Wi-Fi, as I didn't have any in my grottotel (grotty-motel) and managed to do a little work. When Marie arrived, she listened to my story and adventures with intrigue and we chatted for a couple of hours. She caught me up to speed on her life, and as usual, I hung onto every word. Sadly, it had to end and as we were walking to her car, we were laughing about being spotted by someone important. We would have loved to be walking past a set and someone says, "We want you!" We both giggled and agreed that we could keep dreaming, but you never know. The rest of the afternoon went by without any excitement. I wanted to do some more work, so I found a wine bar. They had a very nice wine on for the deal of the day, so I sat outside, as it was warmer than sitting inside with the air conditioning, half watching the world go by, and half working.

I fell into bed happy. Tomorrow would be a new day, new choices, new experiences.

24th October 2019

It was a lovely day. I went to check out the metro, bought tickets for Catalina, had breakfast at the French place, went to Starbucks, and then had a sunset walk on the beach... It was like a dream.

First, I wanted to check out how I was going to get from Long Beach to the bus station near Union Station in LA in a couple of days as I was going to San Francisco. With the amount of luggage I had, I could not just wing it – it was like a military operation! I had to be organised and it was an early start, so I decided it was best in an Uber. Though it pained me to pay for one, it was the easiest, least stressful way to go. Decision made. I then walked to the terminal to get tickets to Catalina

Island as I wanted to make sure I could go and that I was not rushed. It started off in the most bizarre way; I walked up to the counter and this conversation ensued, which amused me no end.

"I would like a ticket to Catalina please." "Do you already have one?" replies the cashier "No, I need a return please."

"So, you already have a ticket?" the cashier replies again. "No, that is why I am asking for a return. Hang on, why did you ask if I had a ticket already?"

"You only need on the way back. Do you have a ticket to get there?" was the reply.

"No, I need both, that is why I need a return ticket," I answer, now getting irritated. The penny finally dropped for me – the difference in buying a return ticket! I always went on the premise that a return ticket is there and back. If I wanted just one way, I would have said that... Clearly, a return ticket to some means just purchasing a ticket for the way back! I managed to buy a ticket for the next day there and back, so I was happy and I got to learn something new!

On my way to the ferry terminal, I had seen the cutest place to stop for a coffee and do some writing, so I headed back there. It was a French place called 'Crème de la Crepe' and was slightly off the beaten track. The lady who was working there was French and had worked for the owner for many years. They had just opened the place after relocating from San Diego. The whole menu looked yummy and the staff were very welcoming, a perfect recipe for a couple of hours work. I loved it. I had a sweet crêpe with mango, strawberries and banana – not intentionally, but it looked so good! It was enormous and was rather delicious. I sat outside with my laptop, enjoying the ambience, sunshine and a rather handsome man sitting next to me.

They let me sit with refills of coffee and water for a couple of hours until I felt it was time to go. So, if ever I go back to Long Beach, that is definitely another stop. I needed to go and do some laundry, so I went back to the motel. On the way back, I stopped at a traffic light and I was aware of a dog panting.

Looking down, I saw the dog and then noticed the owner was on a skateboard. We greeted each other and I asked him how he was. "Not good, I have lost my mobile," he replies. "Oh dear," I respond. He then proceeded to tell me that he thought it fell out of his pocket whilst skateboarding. He was quite calm about it, but I told him that I hoped he finds it as he skated off.

I picked up my dirty clothes and headed to the laundromat. It was like going on an outing! There was a café, a television with a horror movie on, people having dinner, a woman who was the best folder of clothes, and many different people from all walks of life – busily washing, drying, sorting, fluffing and folding. I decided to only do one load of darks then go back to the motel and do my whites as their machines were cheaper, although they did not have a dryer.

After I had done my darks I went to the motel and into the laundry room. Whilst I was trying to figure out how to use the machine, a man walked in. I had noticed him before. He stayed in a room on the ground floor. He was a 'long term' tenant, but very unkempt. I said hello to him and asked him a couple of questions. I immediately regretted it as when he spoke, the smell that came out of his mouth made me want to vomit there and then. Something had clearly died in his mouth, and he had never brushed his teeth. It made it worse that I was in a tight, hot space and he just kept talking. I tried turning away from him, but I could still smell it. Luckily, he did not stay long and nor did I, just in case he came back! Once my washing was all done, I headed out again, this time to the beach. I had thought to myself that I had not been swimming yet. I was right next to the beach, it was 35 degrees Celsius sunshine, and it should not be wasted.

I got my swimsuit on and headed off towards the beach. I was walking down some steps when I heard a voice behind me saying that he was not following me. I looked back and it was the guy who had lost his mobile! He was holding his bike going down the stairs. "Oh, it's you!" he said. Of course I asked him if he had found his mobile, to which he replied that he hadn't. He tells me that he did a jump at the bottom of these stairs, so he had come back without the dog to have a look. He also said that he was worried that if someone found it, they will most probably keep it. He went on to say that there were some real weirdos around. Cue the bearded man literally lying in a prickly bush at the bottom of the stairs, foraging for something.

You could not have made up that scene. He and I had a quick look on the ground, and he points to the man in the bush and says, "See!" We both laughed. I told him again that I hoped that he finds it. He cycled off and I continued to walk to the sea. A few minutes later I heard a noise of something falling to the ground. It was the guy again on the bike path, and whatever was in his pocket fell out. He shouted something to me and we both laughed...

The sand was gorgeous, golden and warm underneath my feet. It was nearing the end of the afternoon, so the sunset glow was coming. There were a few people sunbathing and a couple of people in the water. I decided before I bear my white, larger, wobbly body to the beach goers, I would check how warm the water was. I dipped my feet in and shouted at the top of my voice, "Holy fuck – that is cold!" My sea swimming career ended there and then. There was no way I could go in. How were these other people surviving these temperatures? I took my hat off to them. I kept my body firmly tucked under my clothes and walked instead, enjoying the view, the sound of the waves and warmth on my face. The sun was setting, so the landscape was changing colour, and I realised how lucky I was to be there while pondering about my trip to Catalina in the morning. A while back I pledged that if I walked on a beach, I would pick up at least three pieces of plastic, so they would not enter or re-enter the ocean and pollute it more. The environment is a huge concern for me, and I always try to do what I can to help save and preserve it. I ended up picking up five pieces and walked it to a bin. No effort whatsoever, but an impact nevertheless.

Shenanigans on Catalina Island

Catalina Island turned out to be a whole lot of drama for all of us but in many different ways with very opposing experiences – is this a sign of the times?

October 15th 1958

We got up fairly early with the intention of going to Santa Catalina Island. When I went down to check out the lady said to hurry as the boat bus went in 20 minutes. Janet was there so we dashed upstairs and got our things. Then we hurried along to the bus depot. Gerrie wasn't in the hotel so we gathered she had gone on ahead. However, when we got there she wasn't and anyway the bus had gone. We waited at the depot for a while then returned to the hotel. The clerk checked us back into our old room 1006 and we unchecked all our baggage.

Everyone in the lobby must have seen us go and then return, they must have thought we were crazy! We both fell asleep until about 1.30pm. Gerrie still didn't appear so we concluded she must have caught the bus and perhaps even the boat. We didn't know whether or not to get in touch with the police but decided not to. We kept trying to figure out what we would have done in her place. We decided there was no point in hanging around waiting so after a lot of debating we decided to go to Knott's Berry Farm and Ghost Town. We caught a bus at 3.20pm and got there about 4.00pm. Knott's Berry Farm started off as a little wayside stall selling boysenberries near the silver mining town of Calico. The Knott's have built it up into an enormous concern of shops, bakeries and restaurants. Ghost Town is adjoining to the farm and is really fascinating.

It was a silver rush town which was suddenly deserted. It was left to ruin until the Knott's started to renovate it. It looks exactly as it did in the old Western days. Janet and I loved it. We watched a little old lady on a spinet, we looked in the jail, we watched the blacksmith, we had some boysenberry wine in the bar with its swing doors, we watched a doctors' show, we looked in the old stores and I even had my name printed in the headlines of the local paper and put up on the wall. There was an old gold mine where you could try your luck with the miners. There were a couple of donkeys pulling a grindstone round and round. We both had our photos taken by the latter. When it was nearly dark, we decided to have supper. We went into one restaurant which turned out to be $2.25 chicken dinners only, so we walked out and went to the Calico Grill in Ghost Town. I had a grilled cheese sandwich and boysenberry tart topped with ice cream. Boysenberries are a cross between blackberries and loganberries and are delicious.

After supper we wandered around until 7.30pm when there was a show in one of the bars in old western style with Can-Can girls, a pianist and a singer. The final act was a girl dancing on the counter. You could really get into the atmosphere of the cowboys' days. At 8.15pm there was a melodrama in the Bird Cage Theatre. It had a villain, a maiden in distress and a hero and was part sung and part spoken the audience hissed at the villain and clapped the hero. I enjoyed it. After the play was over, there were these entertainment acts and a croupier who was very amusing. The whole show was very enjoyable. At 9.30pm everything closed so we decided to make tracks home. We got to the bus station and found the last bus had gone. Trust us! The cabs were a fantastic price, so we decided to hitch. We were a bit wary in the dark but there was nothing else we could do. We didn't have to wait long. The man in the car said he would take us to a bus stop, but we got him talking and before we knew it, we were back in LA! He turned out to the son of Campbells Ketchup.

When Janet and I walked into the lobby to our great relief there was Gerrie standing talking to a man. She had booked into a single room and didn't know we still had our old room. It was very lucky we happened to meet. Apparently, she, thinking we had caught the bus, had taken a cab right to the boat ($6.00) and gone over to the island. She was penniless when she arrived so sunbathed on the beach all day without food until it was time for the boat to go. She explained what had happened at the ticket office and they let her go back for free. The same thing with the bus from Wilmington to LA. Thank heavens everything turned out alright.

Over to you Gerrie!

"We rose early. I, as usual was first ready and I took my sleeping bag down to the hotel foyer to wait until Janet and Bella were ready. We were all carrying sleeping bags as we intended to spend the night on the island. Time dragged on, five, ten minutes go by until I decided to go out and buy a film for my camera. I left my bag in someone's care and left. When I returned within ten minutes, the bus had left and apparently the girls had also. I walked out of the foyer and walked to the bus station. There was no mistake, the bus which goes to Long Beach, where the boat leaves for Catalina, had left!

I was in a quandary and after a few moments of indecision, I hailed a taxi to drive me to Long Beach. Needless to say, the fare was expensive and when we reached Long Beach, I found that I only had enough money for a one-way fare. One boat had left for Catalina, I presumed that the girls were on board and bought a ticket, one way for the next boat.

The journey over the water was chilly but rather exhilarating. The boat was relatively small and bobbed a little but to be on the sea after so much travelling on land was pleasantly different. Sailing into Avalon, the main town on the island is worth mentioning. On first appearance the bay looked as though it had been transported from either the South of France or the Caribbean, so glamorous did it look. The sea was a deep blue and the sand was beige, very light and pale. High on one headland off the tiny bay stood a beautiful house. The boat's navigator told us that it belonged to Mr Wrigley, the millionaire of the chewing gum industry. The boat docked, I walked down the wooden wharf and I was on the seafront. The beach was even lovelier than it looked from the boat. Palm trees stood scattered here and there, and small waves rolled onto the sand.

My first thought was to look for Bella and Janet who I thought would be somewhere in Avalon. I wandered around the town for about an hour and decided to sunbathe and consider my situation for it had become! I sat on the beach and ate a raw carrot and celery. I had spent my money on the fare from LA to Long Beach and had only enough left to purchase the one- way ticket to the island. I had no money to return to the mainland or for food and accommodation. I had been relying upon meeting the girls so that money for the return fare could be borrowed but - where were they? They did not seem to be on the island – calamity! Fortunately, my nature, being of the 'no worry' category, I put it out of my mind and continued to swim and sunbathe. All too soon 4.30 came around and it was time for the last boat to leave. I walked with trepidation to the ticket office and presented my story. It sounded ridiculous but plausible and the clerk took pity and issued me a free ticket back to Long Beach.

On the boat once more – at least I was out of that situation. Meanwhile where could the girls have gone? They didn't seem to be on the island, and we had checked out of the hotel in LA that morning. One of my shipboard companions listened with sympathy to my story and offered to take me to dinner. He was on vacation and his home was in Salt Lake City. By the time we reached LA I was ready to eat a house. We went to a restaurant in the city which was unique in that it offered 'all you can eat' for $1.15. I ate enough for one day that evening and as we walked out, I carried a paper bag which contained more food for two or three days more. When I returned to the hotel later in the evening, I checked at the desk to find that the girls had not checked in. I booked a single room in the hotel and said goodbye to my friend. As we stood in the lobby, I saw Janet and Bella walk in and after various explanations found out that they had not been to Santa Catalina and hadn't been able to find out where I had been..."

Gerrie

25th October 2019

I arrived at Catalina Island and it was beautiful! I had taken a bus tour with the obligatory, annoying tour guide, again. This time, she was quite nasally and a terrible actress with scripted jokes. The only ones who laughed were the people who were feeling very embarrassed for her. It was, however, good to do the tour. She gave us a little history of the island and life there.

After the tour I decided to stop for lunch at a lovely beach side restaurant and order a fresh salad as I was craving good, fresh food. Overlooking the very beach mum, Janet and Gerrie had visited, I thought about what was there and what had gone. The second pier which mum mentioned was no longer there, but I was sure that I was looking at the beach they all sunbathed on.

I could understand why they all loved this island so much. Once you get over the tourists, it is spectacular. Only a small percentage of the island is built on, the rest is conserved for the wildlife. Surprisingly, there are Buffalo there. Mum mentioned that they found a safe spot to sleep away from cops and prowlers, but I do not think that they imagined they had to worry about waking up to a buffalo staring at them.

October 16th 1958

Janet and I set off for Catalina and left Gerrie alone in LA. We didn't really like leaving her, but she didn't seem to mind. I went on ahead and got a refund on our tickets back from Knott's Berry Farm. The bus went at 8.40am and Janet just made it. She lost her way on the way back. We sat on the back seat and nearly fell asleep. We caught a boat at 9.45am. It was a very small one with hardly any deck space. I went outside until we left the harbour then again when we neared the island. Catalina is the most beautiful place I have ever seen, especially Avalon, the main town. The bay consisted of two piers where the boats and planes came in and a sandy beach, not too long, with palm trees on it. There were a few shops behind the beach and houses stretching up the hill beyond. The rest of island looked uninhabited.

When we landed, we went straight to the rest room and changed into our bathing costumes. Then we sun-bathed on the beach for most of the rest of the day. It was pretty hot. Near the hundreds I should think. We bought some fruit and celery and sat eating celery sticks on the beach. When the sun went down, we decided to go and have a coffee. Janet got talking to a fat slob who turned out to be a sailor. We had taken our sleeping bags over so that we could sleep out. When we told him this, he offered to let us sleep in his motel room, but we refused. He slopped along in a terrible way and bragged his head off! We got rid of him while we looked around the shops but met him again on the way to supper. He paid for my supper but not Janet's. Why? I don't know. We set off up to this motel and he fixed up Janet's handbag handle for her. Then we said we were going to look for a place to sleep in our sleeping bags. He started off with us but got tired so turned back. Were we pleased! We went back later and bought some cards. Then we sat on the steps of a hotel writing them. A couple of elderly men who were passing stopped to talk to us. They said they were film producers and that they had a yacht. When they heard we were sleeping out they said we could sleep on their yacht. I jumped at the idea. It seemed too good to be true.

He even suggested flying Gerrie out to join us, but we said no. They said they would help us on our travels. They would take us fishing the next day and take us over to the mainland. I had so *many dreams and hopes! They took us up to meet a couple of friends in a very swanky motel. The two men gave us an orange juice each. Whilst they were talking, we discovered they had ulterior motives which they made all too plain. We told them we had changed our minds. I was so disappointed, but I suppose I had been too naïve. Janet said she saw through them and had even waited till I drank my juice to see if it was drugged. Such is life! We set off to find a spot to sleep and after much climbing and scrabbling, found a place under a palm tree on a hill where we thought we would be safe from cops and prowlers.*

The slob had put our things in a locker for us, so we returned to fetch them. Just as we were taking them out two boys came along and started talking to us. We told them what we were doing and one of them offered to let us sleep in his lounge. We were a bit wary this time but agreed. Third time lucky! Their names were Bill and Dick. Bill was the manager of a dairy and it was to his house we went. He shared with his cousin. We sat listening to stereophonic sound hi-fi. Bill went out and the other boy left so we laid on our sleeping bags on the two couches. Bill came back pretty late. He said his cousin would be in later.

We fell asleep before he came but I vaguely woke and saw him put on the lights and stare at Janet. Then he went on through to their room. We laughed when we could imagine his face on seeing two girls asleep in his lounge.

October 17th 1958

Bill left at 7.00am. I heard him go but fell asleep again. When we finally got up, Ray, the cousin, called out that breakfast was ready. He was really good-looking and very nice. So was Bill. Ray had to go out while we were still eating. We washed up our own plates and a huge pile of theirs. Ray returned while we were washing up and we had quite a long chat with him. He had also had quite a life. He had even lived with gypsies for a couple of years. He gave us each a little pocketbook and biro for washing up which was thoughtful but quite unnecessary because we were paying him for having us. We also did their bed and generally tidied up. He said we could leave all our belongings at their house while we were sightseeing and use it whenever we wished. He walked halfway up to the bird garden with us then we said goodbye. There were some lovely birds there but the most interesting were the Mina birds. They all had a long repertoire, one even wolf whistled. We were quite flattered until we realised what it was! We must have sat for half an hour talking back at them. One sounded exactly like a very old man.

25th October 2019

The bird garden sanctuary has gone and is now actually a pre-school. It was shut down as the birds seemed to procreate too much and they were over run, and the costs were huge. Most of the birds were shipped to the LA zoo. Sitting there, I was looking up at the Wrigley house that they would have seen, but of course it has changed, and it is now a bed and breakfast called 'Casa Ada'.

October 17th 1958

When we were outside again, we hailed a passing man on his bike and asked him where the road on up past the bird garden went. He said nowhere and that he was just going to pick wild figs. We jumped at that idea and he said we could join him.

He had a box, so we got one from a nearby fire station. Then we ducked under some barbed wire and made our way across waste shrubland and undergrowth. It would have been a hunter's paradise as there were thousands of quail everywhere. Every step you took disturbed hundreds of them. We felt as though we were on a deserted treasure island surrounded by palm trees and wildlife. It was so peaceful. The man was a sailor, a very nice character. He had a bull terrier! He showed us which were the ripe figs and the difference between the various types. He kept on giving us ones to try which we didn't like to refuse until we thought we would be running all day!

We didn't pick too many as we had to carry them back to LA. We walked back down halfway with him then he carried on, on his bike as he had an inspection. We took it in turns to carry the box on our heads native-like until we nearly got back to Bill and Rays house. Then I suddenly remembered, I had left my sunglasses in the restroom at the bird garden. I had to traipse all the way back in the boiling heat, a mile there and a mile back. Luckily, they were still there. We wandered around the town buying cards etc. At three o'clock we took a trip on a glass bottomed boat. It was $1.75 and lasted three quarters of an hour. It was quite interesting but not worth the money! Our boat back to the mainland left at 4.00pm and our boat got in at 3.50pm. Then the trouble started. We honed it back to Bill's house and grabbed our belongings. We didn't even have time to leave a note. Then we dashed back to the pier just in time to see the boat leave. We were absolutely pooped so we just sat on a beach and gawped at the disappearing boat.

Several people realised what had happened and spoke to us. We had been saying all day shall we stay on another day or not, then when we missed the boat. We began to think of every possible way of getting back. We tried to get hold of the harbour master to see if there were any private boats back. We spoke to several people *and in the end, a lady in a wheelchair and a man got us over to the plane. The lady came with us and spoke to the ticket man. He let us go with our boat tickets and told us to speak to the ticket people at the other end. The fare should have been another $3.00 each, which we didn't have. A local hotel manager who heard our predicament offered to take us halfway back to LA in his car. When we said goodbye to Mrs Butts, we boarded the plane which was rolling very precariously in the sea. We seemed to be almost sitting in the sea when we sat down. We set off with a deafening roar and bumped like h—- 'til we were in the air. It was quite a thrill for Janet and I. We left Catalina outlined in a blazing red sunset. I do hope I go back sometime. We flew very low over the sea but gained height when we reached Long Beach. We could see the swimming pools in all the gardens below and also a hill covered in oil wells outlined by the sunset. When we landed a young couple came up to us and said they had overheard our predicament and would take us right back to our hotel. We accepted, then told the manager. I hope he wasn't hurt. We went to the ticket office and they said we needn't bother to pay the extra. Needless to say, we were pretty pleased.*

The couple were very nice and as usual, very interested in our trip. When we got back, we exchanged stories. Gerrie had been to Knott's Berry Farm and Disneyland. In the end we all then went to Catalina.

25th October 2019

At the restaurant, I ordered an avocado and shrimp salad – It was brought to me swiftly and it was delicious. I accompanied the salad with a glass of rosé and sat back to enjoy.

I overheard a couple beside me ask about the history of something on the island and the waiter stopped and spoke to them for about five minutes answering their question, chatting away. Through the buzz of my rosé and confidence of my author status, I thought he was perfect to ask my own question. So, when he came over, I smiled and asked, "Do you know if the restaurant is where the second pier used to be?" Expectantly waiting for the same response as the other couple, he replied, "No," and walked off!

Oh, I thought to myself… I sat there a little longer and he came back asking if I wanted another glass of wine. "No thanks, but I would like a coffee," I replied. He nodded in acknowledgment and sauntered off. Five minutes… Seven minutes… Ten minutes later and not a coffee bean in sight. I watched for the waiter busy going around all the tables asking if the other guests needed anything else. One table said they wanted another beer. I was unable to catch his eye until a couple of minutes later when he gave the man his beer! I was so angry… I beckoned him over and told him to forget the coffee. He said that he was just about to get it, but I knew that was a blatant lie. It was only a drip coffee – so it consisted of a cup, coffee jug, pour and deliver. It was not a cappuccino or anything that took time. I asked for the check and left the exact cash. I did not leave a tip and when I passed him, he did not even say goodbye. Okay, I thought…shit happens.. After my lunch, I headed to the museum to see if I could find anymore history about the island.

Sadly, the museum police – this woman at the desk, got in the way of any plans. I asked if there was anyone I could speak to and explained what I wanted, about my mum and the book. She showed me to the bookshelf and told me I could find all the information in there. After a while of rifling through these books getting pissed off as I was wasting the little time I had on the island, I told her I did not have time to go through all the books. So she told me to Google the information. I think I just stared at her before leaving. Not a pleasant experience overall at all, I was most disappointed with the museum. I felt a little down, the buzz of the rosé had worn off, so I needed sugar... Ice cream! I bought an overpriced ice cream and headed off to the beach where I sat and waited until it was time to board the boat. The boarding situation was a complete joke – unless you had paid for premium seating, you were required to stand in the heat with no shade or anywhere to sit... Boy, were we reminded that we were on economy tickets. And no kind people with airplanes insight.

I could totally see why mum thought it was paradise. In a postcard home, she described it as:

"This place is just heaven, just like the South of France. There is one palm tree lit up at night. It is so warm you can wander around in a bathing suit at midnight. As the tourist season is over it is very peaceful and there is plenty of space on the beach."

Sadly, my experience on Catalina Island was not as positive as mums, and I think it was awesome that she ended her piece of heaven in such a fabulous fashion. I would love to go back, but I would buy premium tickets, stay overnight, avoid the museum and eat elsewhere! It certainly looked like paradise. It was just a shame it did not deliver the sentiment.

Whistle Stop Tour of San Francisco

26th October 2019

Sitting on a bus from LA to San Francisco, I glanced over at the couple next to me who took out some boiled sweets to eat. A memory popped into my head of when we used to travel in the car with mum, and we would have 'travel sweets'. They were an actual tin of boiled, fruity sweets, covered in icing sugar. Now, instead of travel sweets, I have eaten mouthfuls of popcorn and a blueberry muffin! Oh, how times have changed but it makes me smile at the thought and memory.

They were such a cute couple in their 70s, from Italy. They held hands or chatted away to each other most of the way. My heart melted and I said to the universe, "That is going to be me one day!"

October 07th 1958

None of us slept very much and were all fully conscious at dawn. There was one period of driving during the night when Bill had to be careful to avoid driving over skunks. Another time we felt an awful bump on the car which Bill said was a dog he had run over. It ran into the car. He wouldn't stop as he said he must have killed it outright. When we entered California, we had to go through an inspection station looking for fruit and veggies. We had some fruit which we hid but completely forgot about the Kelley's potatoes and carrots. Bob said we hadn't anything then the inspector looked in the other bag on the floor. We felt a bit silly when he said, "What's this?"

He then asked if we had any sweet potatoes, which we hadn't. So, he let us through. We would have liked to have taken the Redwood route, but the boys were in a hurry, so we went via Sacramento. We arrived over an enormous bridge which we thought was the Golden Gate but which we later discovered was the Bay Bridge. The boys took us to the YM where they also checked in. We only had to pay $1.50 each. I really enjoyed the ride and was quite sorry when we arrived. We thanked the boys and went up to our room.

About half an hour later Bill rang and asked if we would like to go for a run in the car. We jumped at it. They said that they would pick us up in an hour. We hired an iron for 35c and all had showers. We felt really scruffy after travelling for over 24 hours. I don't think the boys recognised us when we walked into the lobby in dresses instead of jeans and desert boots! We drove down to Fisherman's Wharf where all the small fishing boats were, and the fish stands and souvenir shops. There was a boat trip around the harbour at 4.00pm which we decided to take. The boys paid. The boat went quite near to the Golden Gate Bridge for us to get a good look at. Next it circled around Alcatraz, the State Penitentiary for incorrigibles on a little island in the bay. It is almost fool-proof from escapes. We imagined we would see groups of gangs of men in chains but there were no signs of life. The place fascinated me. Next the boat went under the Bay Bridge. To me it looked just as amazing as the Golden Gate. After the trip we were going to have supper at the Wharf but decided it was too expensive so we went onto Chinatown. We cruised around looking for a parking place for ages until we gave it up as a bad job, returned the car to the YM and took a taxi (staying at the YMCA sounds terrible but it was a YMCA Hotel for men, women and children). Chinatown is a wonderful place. It is the largest outside the Orient. You really get into the atmosphere there. It was really fascinating. Our stomachs were just about eating our throats by then, so we went straight in and ordered a family dinner for five. There was enough food for at least ten. We couldn't eat half of it. We ended the meal with China tea and Chinese fortune cookies. They are hollow shell shaped cookies with your fortune written inside. When we couldn't possibly force another mouthful down, we wandered around the stores looking for souvenirs. On the spur of the moment we decided to go into a Chinese film. It was quite an experience. We couldn't understand a word! Gerrie and Bob fell asleep. We stayed for about an hour then left. It was getting on by then, so we caught a taxi back.

It was certainly quite an eventful day. We worked out how much money we owed the boys. They refused to take any, so we went up to their room and shoved an envelope in. Their room was 841 and ours was 1141. We thought they would probably be mad with us but just as Janet and I got back to our room they were ringing Gerrie to see if we would go out the following night.

26th October 2019

My welcome back to San Francisco did not start too well and it was all in the name of research. I found myself being scared shitless without planning to be. After I dropped my luggage and checked into my hotel, I decided to go and investigate where the YMCA was, where mum and the girls stayed, and to walk around the area, getting some nostalgia. It was getting dark but still light enough, so I did not think too much about it. I had found myself in many of the dodgy downtowns with the undesirables and to get through them, I was aware of my surroundings and I kept alert... But this was a whole different level. I got to what is known as the Tenderloin area, in particular, Turk Street. The clock said 5.30 pm, but it felt like something out of a horror movie. It suddenly became darker as I got closer and the buzz of locals and tourists died out. I was walking down Turk Street on my own and realised I was not in a good area. Not only were there homeless people, the usual tents and trash, and people passed out, there were others smoking crack, meth and shooting up heroin just there, in front of me. People were spaced out, high, and drunk, doing drug deals, I did not feel safe at all. I was carrying a lot of worth in my backpack, my passport, cash, laptop, and jewelry (It was not always safe to leave them in hotel rooms and if I had known the area, I would not have taken anything with me).

It was so uncomfortable having to stop at red lights to wait to cross so eventually I ignored them and kept walking (even though I could have got a fine), as I was worried someone would grab my bag, mug me or harm me. I knew I was being watched too. I walked with confidence, making sure that I did not look like someone who was vulnerable, even though every vein and cell in my body felt it. My heart was pounding, and I thought everyone could hear it. I was sweating and my legs felt like jelly. I found the building after what felt like an eternity and I very quickly took out my phone, took two photos and found my way out. After walking a little further, I found people to walk with – families, couples or people who looked safer (They did not know I was walking with them).

I eventually got out and into safer streets. Someone had recommended a place for dinner, so I went. Three large glasses of red wine later, I felt a little better! Then the bill came… How? How can one person spend so much on a dinner? The food was minimal but when you add three glasses of wine, tax and tip, I had paid for a village to eat for a week. I certainly did not intend to spend that much money as that was nearly half of my weekly budget! But I had scrimped and saved up as it was the anniversary of mum's death – so I spoilt myself.

October 08th 1958

We got the desk to call us at 7.30, then we set out for Chinatown again. We wanted to have a longer look around. We caught a cable car which was most precarious. San Francisco consists of a series of steep hills like switch backs. The cars are pulled up by underground cables. It was quite an experience. They seemed so old fashioned.

We wandered up and down Chinatown then walked down to Market Street, one of the main shopping areas. There we went completely crazy. Janet and Gerrie bought dresses and I bought Bermuda shorts, pants and a beige lambswool sweater. We starve ourselves then buy unnecessary clothes! We then caught another cable car to Fisherman's Wharf where we had a longer look around.

We just got back at 6.30pm in time to meet the boys. They had their sailor's uniforms on and really looked something! We hurriedly changed. We walked down to Market Street to see Liz Taylor in 'A Cat on a Tin Roof'. It was very good. Unfortunately, we went in the middle. After the show we went for a coffee. Then we returned to the hotel and sat talking in the lobby for a time. We got someone to take our photos for us. They were returning back to their base the next day, so we said goodbye.

27th October 2019

I woke up feeling very excited, like a kid at Christmas – I was spending the whole day with a friend of mine. We met a couple of years ago when we were both living in Vienna. She has been and continues to be a huge source of support, and we have great fun together. Her name is Linda and she is originally from San Francisco but has been in Vienna for the last couple of years but circumstances had taken her back, lucky for me.

She picked me up from my hotel at around 09.00 in her no-frills truck – not even power steering. I was certainly not complaining… We both giggled knowing we were going to be in for a fun-filled day.

First stop was to seek out the lions in Golden Gate Park where mum and the girls had their photos taken. Who knew the park had so many lions! We thought we found them, but they were not so Spanish looking (as mum had described), more like Sphinx looking. A quick photo was taken… Certainly not of me on top of one – much nicer without! Next was to the Japanese Gardens which looked lovely but because time was not on our side, we decided it was not worth paying the entrance fee. The museum would have taken too long, so we sat that one out, too. Instead, we just had a glimpse, agreed they were beautiful and moved on. Next, we headed to Ocean Beach and Cliff House. En route we went down the famous Lombard Street which was pretty scary especially as Linda told me her truck was like 50 years old and she was not sure how good the breaks were! We laughed at the thought that the tourists would soften the impact if we lost control and crashed!

There were tourists everywhere, all in the road taking photos and selfies, all from different countries. So not only did we have to navigate the tight turns and steepness of the hill, we also had to avoid the people. We safely got down and continued. We arrived at Cliff House, which was where mum went exploring on her own. She left the other two back on the beach. It looked like quite a long walk up a steep hill, but it was worth it for mum. Cliff House is now a restaurant and I think the only original part left was the sign on top of the building. We both decided we were hungry, so we stopped off for a bite to eat and a chat. Next was just touring around, seeing Alcatraz from the land, the Golden Gate Bridge, and the steep hills that San Fran had to offer. I would tell stories of the time that I was there with mum back in October 2006, to the actual day. It had of course changed so much since then it was hard to recognise. I have such fond memories and realise how lucky I am to have them.

October 2006

Mum and I had met in San Francisco, as it was a stop off for me coming home from New Zealand where I had been living for a couple of years, before we headed to Las Vegas. We stayed in the Holiday Inn near to Fisherman's Warf. We were typical tourists and wandered around Fisherman's Warf, and we went to Pier 39 to see (and smell) the sea lions. They were also very loud! Then we went to book tickets to Alcatraz. Unfortunately, there happened to be a strike on so we could not go on that day and the next day was nearly full.

The only time left was on the last boat so we took that one. It was a shame that we could not stay too long on Alcatraz, we did not want to find ourselves stuck there for the night! It was fascinating though, seeing where the prisoners slept, ate, exercised, and the view they saw back on the mainland. The audio tour included prisoners recounting their experiences and life on Alcatraz. We saw the head made of concrete used to fool the guards on the night of the only escape in the history of the prison – though there were many attempts. On the boat, mum of course mentioned her trip back in 1958 when they went on the boat but of course they did not get off as there were prisoners still occupying the island. It was so special doing this trip with mum and her going down memory lane. We went down Lombard Street which was super cool as it was just like the movies.

Then of course we went on the famous trolleys that take you up and down the steep hills to save your legs. We managed to have both experiences of sitting on a seat and hanging off the side, which was quite exhilarating. Next stop, Union Square and we sat and had a coffee while watching people and chatting. Enjoying the moment, we agreed that we were very lucky to have these travels and make such wonderful memories. The day came that we were to go over the Golden Gate bridge.

As I sit here writing about it, I am laughing and smiling through tears. It was such a happy memory. The next day, we decided to hire some bikes to cycle over. We found a rental place and picked up the bikes. To get up to the bridge there was quite a steep bit to cycle up. I puffed and panted, and got my legs working to make it up, but mum walked with her bike. Once we got up on the bridge, she did not feel comfortable to cycle as there were many people around, so she walked the whole bridge with her bike! I was cycling away, back and forth to check on her and I was giggling to myself. She wanted to tell people that she had cycled. So, at the end of the bridge, I got out my camera and she got on her bike, wobbling away towards me whilst I snapped away. We managed to get one decent photo. With this short cycle, she had gained confidence and we grabbed our bikes and cycled further.

We ended up in a seaside town and a wooded area. I remember that we were in awe of the fantastically huge trees. We spent a whole day exploring until it was time to return the bikes and head off for a large glass of wine. We spent only three days in San Francisco, but we had such a good time. We then flew to Las Vegas for a few days to go back to San Fran to catch a flight back to London.

October 09th 1958

Called at 7.30 am again. We set off for the post office to collect our mail. I had a couple of letters which we sat and read outside. There was a long list of 'wanted' men and women in the post office with photos and descriptions. It was fascinating looking at them all. Then we caught a bus out to the Golden Gate Park. It is a beautiful place, one of the biggest and best laid out in the country. We each took photos sitting on a lion outside the museum which looked really Spanish. Then we looked around the Japanese tea gardens. It was such a beautiful day we nearly didn't go into the museum but decided we had better.

It was also very interesting. We carried on in the bus to the beach known as Ocean Beach. The ride was interesting as you can easily see the Spanish influence in the houses. They are well set out, clean streets. There was an atmosphere of peace and prosperity. Knob Hill is one of the most famous points where all the wealthy people live. At the beach we changed into swimsuits in a bowling alley. We spent the rest of the day sunbathing. I had two swims, but the water was pretty cold and terribly rough. Bathing was really prohibited. The beach stretched for as far as you could see one way and ended in rocks the other way. At the end of the day I walked up to Cliff House, a souvenir shop and restaurant, a well- known spot. The other two stayed behind. We went back on the cable cars and spent the evening writing letters etc. We had supper at the Y. It was a really enjoyable day.

27th October 2019

After exploring, Linda and I thought it would be a good time to park the truck, grab some lunch and go on the trolleys. We first went to a suggested spot for some lunch but there was a game on the TV screens, so it was busy. They sat us on a horrible table, I asked to move, which they did very begrudgingly. We sat there looking at the menu and then looked at each other and thought it was best to go – the staff had been rude, it was noisy, and clearly, we were not going to get much service. We found a Mexican place with gorgeous views. Sadly, the views were really the only good thing about it. The sangria tasted like petrol mixed with vinegar, the food was poor, and it lacked atmosphere, so we ate and ran. Off to the trolley stop we went. Linda knew of this great trick to get the best views of San Francisco whilst riding the trolley! All the tourists wanted to sit on the sides or hang off the side but (I am giving a secret away here) if you stand at the back outside with the man who collects the tickets, you get unobstructed views and it is breathtaking! We got chatting to the ticket man who thought I was an Instagram influencer! Ha ha, Linda was clearly my manager… We did not want to disappoint him.

We took the trolley to Union Square and decided to get a glass of champagne. We struggled to find somewhere and ended up in a department store overlooking the square, not having champagne but a glass of pretty horrible wine, but at least we could chat some more and watch life in the square.

We were very aware of the time as I had to catch a bus to start my journey to Seattle. We finished up and took a sunset trolley back to the truck. The bus stop was at pier 39 so we drove there, and I was dropped off in time to get on my bus. The bus ride was great as it took us to the financial district where I had not been before. Although it was late, and the streets were deserted, I liked the look of it and wanted to come back to San Francisco to explore more.

I had a fabulous day and I was so lucky to have Linda with me. The journey has been quite lonely, so it was nice to be able to experience things with someone else. Thanks Linda!

Journey from Hell

27th October 2019

I had been very lucky with my travel apart from the blip catching the bus at Seaport in San Diego but on this day, I experienced a journey I hope to never encounter or go through again. This was to be the biggest journey to date. A bus from San Francisco to Emeryville, then a wait of around 30 minutes before jumping on a train to Seattle. The total journey should have taken around 23 hours. Well now... I thought it was going to be a fun way to see more of California – a little of Oregon and Washington. I thought that I was going to sleep when I could watch movies I had downloaded, and that I was going to write a positive review of my journey. I am guessing you kind of know how my life goes by now... There's always a hitch! Sit back, grab a glass of wine (oh, that's me!) and I shall tell you about my journey from the depths, where giant squid live.

Before I boarded the bus, I was receiving texts to say that the train was late departing. No biggie, it is only for an hour. Then the second text comes in, and it is delayed for an extra half an hour, so we are behind schedule already. That is okay, I thought, a couple of hours was no big deal. The bus journey was good, as mentioned already, very smooth and to be honest, I was enjoying it as I was getting a tour of San Francisco at night. We arrived at 9.30 pm to the train station and we were told that the train was late, and they were not sure how late it was going to be. I tried to check in my luggage. When it was weighed, it was a combined weight of 111 lbs. Um... What? I think back to see if I remembered that I had accidentally packed a small human, piece of furniture or weight belt, but no. So, I had no clue what this phenomenon of growing luggage was! I had not bought anything as I could not afford it, so still no clue! Eventually, we heard the best news – the train was arriving at 11.39 pm. We were herded like school children and lined up on the platform, with some people going to the sleeping carriages, and some to business class then the coach class. I had paid a little extra and had gone business class. More space and the last time I did the same, we got free coffee and snacks, and it was quite pleasant. The sleeping carriages were double the price and I could not spend that much, so I compromised with business class.

We were told whilst waiting the reason for the two-hour delay was because they had to change the toilet carriage as they had a problem, then there was a signal failure. We got on the train and I found my seat next to the window. The steward was very courteous and friendly and gave me a bottle of water. I sat back to relax and enjoy.

Twenty minutes later, the emergency brakes slammed on and we came to a halt. We stood there for 30 minutes then an hour, two hours... Time was ticking on. I saw some cops go by the train with flashlights and thought that they were looking for immigrants, or a stowaway or something. Then I overheard a conversation from some other passengers who mentioned that we had hit a car. They said the car was stopped on the tracks with no one inside. Shit! I hoped that we were going to get on the move soon.

I was sitting waiting when I heard another passenger say, "Ask her, she may have one." So, this young guy asked if I had a phone charger. I did, so I lent it to him, and he was so grateful otherwise he would not have been able to call an Uber when he got to his destination. Emergency diverted for that one! I was not tired enough to sleep so I started chatting with the young guy, another man and his mother. It turned out that the young guy was training to be a hacker, and the older one was building software against the hacking. It was something straight out of a movie… We got chatting and managed to while away some time. At one stage, a conductor came around and he confirmed that we had hit a car and there were dead bodies, but he would not indulge us further.

We had been sitting for over four hours and the 'kind, courteous steward' was now curled up on a seat trying to sleep. No water or information had been given to us and the power was intermittently going out, so the toilets were not always flushing, and the air conditioning was not always on – I was beginning to know what cattle felt like. We were told to go into the lounge room if we wanted to continue talking by our 'kind, courteous steward' so she could sleep. It was clear, in an emergency we knew who we could rely on!

We went into the lounge room and talked some more… Four hours… Five hours… Still waiting… I was then shown a Twitter feed which showed that three people had died in the car. Shit! I also overheard that the train was damaged, so they needed to replace the engine car. The driver who witnessed it was sent home due to stress and we were all waiting without word, water, food or even kind words to ask if we are okay. The car had been trying to race the train over the crossing, but the train won. A few other people who were in the sleeping carriages had no clue what was going on as they had been tucked up in bed. They came and asked us what had happened. Finally, at around 7.00am we were back on our way. I later learnt that although the service had been appalling, at least I was on the train as many people were stranded at the train terminals, having to sleep on the cold, concrete floors! As we were bumbling along, we got an announcement over the intercom that breakfast was served but with a limited service, as we did not know how long we would have power. I went to the dining cart and was told to sit down like a school child. I was sitting there looking at the breakfast menu really not wanting anything, so I just asked for a coffee. I was thrown out of the dining cart and told to go downstairs to get one from the café cart. I had to pay for the coffee and a bun …So much for my free snacks and coffee.

I was getting more pissed off, and I was so tired as I had only slept for about 20 minutes. The reason I have not stayed in hostels is because I hate snoring and boy, were there some loud ones on the train. The sound of the engine was more soothing than the sound of someone's lungs getting tied up and pulled out of their mouths. Then they stopped breathing for a second, then a grunt… I put my iPod on to drown out the noise and tried to get some more sleep. I snoozed a little more until we got to Sacramento. We dropped passengers off and put more on, then we waited… And waited, again. The power was switched off and the announcement came that again, the toilets were not going to flush. Oh, boy… Have you ever been on an airplane overnight flight? The morning bodily functions… Need I say more? I think we sat at the station for just under two hours… I got the news that we were ten hours behind schedule. Still no water given (you can buy some or drink the most disgusting stuff from a little tap), no apology, and no information given. My 'kind, courteous steward' was still trying to stay away from us and our complaints by hiding under her coat!

There was a strong aroma of body odour oozing out of my neighbour, which was not pleasant as it kept wafting my way. There were also the 'duck hunters' with their oversized bellies, American flag tank tops, long greying hair, and not a lot of teeth. There was the American vet, who was very upset as he had diabetes, and he wanted and needed healthy food, not café cart crap. People from all walks of life and cultures made up the passenger list. Some were more patient than others. We got moving again and I was rewarded by a beautiful sunrise overlooking a body of water. It was stunning and temporarily I was reminded of how excited I was to see the landscape of the West Coast. I spent the next few hours in and out of consciousness as I was so tired. In between, I watched what I very smartly downloaded as we did not have Wi-Fi. I decided not to spend the money on lunch in the dining cart but used a voucher I was given for the total sum of $6 instead. Off. I trotted to the café cart and bought a plastic, microwavable – and I am sure it would glow in the dark – hot dog. I eventually went into the dining cart and enquired what time dinner was. I was told that we would not get food until all the sleepers had theirs, and only if there was any food left over. I had by this time been on the train for almost 20 hours. I spoke to others and the mood on the train was one of anger, disdain, panic, and fear.

Not one of the staff seemed to give a shit. I still didn't know what time I was due to arrive in Seattle. As I sat, I watched the faces and body language of others walking past my seat to the dining cart, and then the reaction of them walking back past me – most of them passed with a big sigh and no one looked happy. Communities were forming out of annoyance and people were chatting to strangers.

There was the underlying knowing of how we were all feeling in the business and coach seats. We were separated to the sleepers, so they may have been having a jolly old time. Well, they were certainly well fed! I managed to find a conductor and asked him what time we are due to get into Seattle. He told me that the plan was to go to Portland and then we would all get on a bus to ride the rest of the way. The train was apparently still having issues and it would be quicker to bus us than keep us on the train.

We are due into Portland between 1.30 am and 2.30 am, so I was to arrive in Seattle around 5.00 am. An announcement came on to say that we were all getting a free meal to apologise for the inconvenience of the delay... Well, you can imagine the rapturous, joyous celebrations that emulated out of the carriages. Nope, all I could hear were crickets. It was a military exercise, we were not allowed to move until we were called. The sleepers got first dibs and we got the leftovers, it seemed.

Around an hour later, our car was called to the dining car. I eagerly went in thinking we would be getting steak and fries, but we were given what looked like prison food, beef stew and a lump of hard mashed potato. I was the only one who had taken wine in with me (which I had purchased for 'medicinal purposes') as I thought it would be a leisurely affair – dining with the others, chatting and laughing about our experience so far. No, I think we were faster than McDonalds. In and out before we could say, "Boo!" Very disappointing. So, I sat back down, drank my red wine, and watched a movie. We finally arrived in Portland and were shuffled onto a bus whose driver clearly had been told that we were all pissed off and behind time so get us to Seattle as quickly as possible. Well, I think he thought he was driving a supercar, not a clapped-out old bus. He pushed it to the point that the gears got stuck when we had to stop for traffic. Luckily, they held out and we eventually arrived into Seattle over 13 hours late. What felt like two days of my life had passed, but I was finally there!

* Since writing this, the train company was given my experience and gave me a full refund and an apology from the kind representative on behalf of the company, over the telephone. All is forgiven!

Seattle – Signs Are Everywhere

29th October 2019

I arrived in what felt like Siberia! It was a beautiful morning but fucking cold. When I packed back in Vienna, my thoughts were that I was going to stay in LA for the duration of the time and although I had packed for every emergency and 'just in case', I did not think l would be entering a proper winter. My open-toed wedges, off the shoulder flowery top and light jacket just didn't work. I did manage to bring a couple of jumpers, but I had to wear at least three of them to feel warm enough outside! I sure hoped that I would get over the shock.

I arrived at my Airbnb via Uber with a very knowledgeable driver who told me a little about how the state of Washington is divided. I listened with interest whilst getting a glimpse of Seattle. I held my breath as the morning sunshine danced in the sea and sparkled off the buildings into a spectacular show of colours and lighting up the array of trees. I had arrived deep into the American fall and it did not let me down.

I was going to go to Seattle back in January, but I decided not to. It was always a place I wanted to come and here I was! Oh, universe... I clearly manifested this... It would have been nicer to have a healthier bank account but hey, that was also being manifested! Seeing the American fall colours had been a dream of mine. That was something I would not have seen if I had stayed in LA, so I was super grateful that I was experiencing and seeing it. I was so pleased when I got to my Airbnb. It did not disappoint; it was the cutest guest house at the end of someone's garden. It was warm, had a full kitchen and a huge TV! Oh, the universe kept on delivering! The first thing I did was have a shower. I had not showered or brushed my teeth for over 48 hours – I had officially taken on a caveman persona. My hair looked like I was something from a different dimension, my teeth felt like they had grown a layer of plaque, and my eyes were red and swollen. I probably smelt strange too. I emerged from the shower feeling more normal. I looked down at my stomach and I was sure I had something growing inside – it was huge! I felt like a blob. I had been living off shit food for the last few weeks as I had not had anywhere to cook.

So, as my luggage weight grew so did my body weight! The organic, healthy food days were a distant memory. It had been supermarket convenience food with more sugar, salt, saturated fat and calories than the population of the US. I had a snooze and then went to the supermarket. I got very excited picking up a pepper and putting it into my basket. I love to cook, and prefer it over having fast food, so this was heaven for me. I spent at least an hour roaming around (okay, I kept getting lost!) and I filled my basket. I was a happy cookie.

31st October 2019

My morning started with a dollop of fear. I had to sort out some banking issues. Every time I went onto my back account, my heart started racing and I experienced so much anxiety. However, no matter how much I budgeted, shit happened behind the scenes and there were unexpected surprises, and not of the celebration kind. One issue of moving around the world so often is having problems with mobile phones and sim cards. If you actually live somewhere then it is cool, you get your phone and sim card and a package which suits your lifestyle and you do not have to think too much more about it. But if you are like me then it gets tricky. I have a European sim card (that was where I was last a proper resident!) but when I came to the US, I got a local one which helped with texting, data, etc. But my bank accounts, messaging services, etc. are all registered with my European one. When I arrived, I turned off my data roaming for my European mobile but that did not work, so I ended up with a € 180 bill! I took my sim card out altogether and only turned it on when needed. It was surprises like that I could do without, thank you very much. When you have a business, you need a steady number. But if you are a digital nomad then as I say, it gets tricky. I could not let this fear get any bigger, so I grabbed my laptop and went exploring.

Oh, Starbucks, same décor and atmosphere, just different state and town... The chilled music adding to the ambience. This really annoying man with his laptop prop was talking to anyone who sat next to him, whether they wanted to or not. He kept apologising to this poor girl for not letting her get on with work but talked to her anyway. It was not a conversation; it was him talking at her. Often, people are too polite to say anything, as was she. Even when he went off and she put her earphones in. When he came back, he continued where he left off, so she took her earphones out, but he didn't seem to care! I was giggling to myself watching this.

Laptops were part of the décor on each table, but this was an affluent area of Seattle, so there were yummy mummies, yogis, businessmen and other locals all getting their morning coffee. The God squad sat down for a refreshment but left to continue their mission to convert people. Outside the window there was a crocodile line of pre-schoolers dressed up in their Halloween costumes going back for lunch after a run in the park. There was a dragon, fireman, princess, minion, and tiger, all proudly showing off their costumes. It was cuteness overload.

I was really looking forward to being part of Halloween in the city. I found myself in a family-orientated area so it will be busy with kids running from house to house, thrusting their buckets eagerly watching how much candy is going in, their eyes getting larger and larger. The parents with nervous looks on their faces knowing that they were in for a week of sugar highs but also looking forward to indulging in some partying themselves after they got home.

I remember Halloween as a child. Back in the UK it was not really celebrated yet, however, as mum owned a card and gift shop and a lot of her customers were American who celebrated, she had to supply their demands. If you cannot beat them, you join them, so we would also have Halloween parties, which were really special. I think it was mum's way of being as gory as she could 'legally' be. She made up a game where we had to be blindfolded and put our hands into bowls with different textures. They would be body parts or fluids. For example, dried coconut for fingernails, peeled grapes for eyeballs, and jelly for brains... It was great fun! Friends of ours loved coming to these 'unusual' parties. Mum loved any celebration or holiday and would always make a big fuss. I have now taken over that sentiment. Trick or treating in our neighbourhood was funny, as no one was prepared for us. The homeowners did not know what we were doing. They would open the door, nervously, to find us all dressed up, shouting 'trick or treat' then begging for sweets along with a dog. We were given all sorts of stuff from money to pie and when they ignored us and did not answer, we would do a trick. We would stick Sellotape over their doorbell so it would continuously ring or throw toilet paper around the garden. We were given pumpkin pie once and when I tried it, I nearly threw up! We thanked them for it and left. Once out of sight of the owners, I handed my piece to my dog who was a food-hoover (food-vacuum-cleaner) and he refused it, too! That is how bad it was! Oh, good memories though.

Starbucks kept delivering and of course, the next person who walked in was a woman holding her cat with a Perspex carrier on her back as a backpack. Normal, of course... Then the teenagers, some dressed in their costumes, oh no, hang on – they are just in their onesies... I finally peeled myself away from the goings-on in Starbucks and walked to a lake to see the view. It was pretty stunning, but I felt that if I stood there too long, my body would start rigor mortis as it is so cold, so I walked home.

On the walk home there was the air of excitement and anticipation for the events taking place. It reminded me of Christmas. Some houses had clearly been decorated for weeks as their pumpkins had started to decay, and the candy on the supermarket shelves had nearly all gone. I, of course, wanted to go out and experience this phenomenon. After the sun went down, I donned my hat, scarf, two jumpers and coat, and headed out. I could already hear the screeching of laughter, and that was just the adults meeting their friends! What made me giggle the most were the fathers who were dressed up, clearly under duress from the kids, drinking a beer and chatting to their friends with this unspoken acknowledgment that they looked ridiculous. There were Buzz Lightyears, a thigh master, dragons, Woody, some were just in hats along with an array of other home-made costumes which delighted their kids. Laughter and shouts of 'trick or treat' filled the air. The sky was a blaze of red, purple, orange, yellow and blues as the sun went down, then the coloured lights from the Halloween decorations lit up the neighbourhood. It was all good fun for both the kids, parents and homeowners… Next on the list… Thanksgiving.

01st November 2019

I am sitting writing this after I have just booked the last step of my journey – spending a month in Vancouver. I might have to buy a warmer coat! I thought back to 2016 and noted that Vancouver, for both mum and I, had a huge significance.

Their adventure began in Vancouver and mine began there too, but in a completely different way. I think back to June 2015, when I quit my job, sold my London flat and booked a one-way (it was actually a return ticket 'just in case') flight to Vancouver. I must add that I did not know why I chose Vancouver. It just sounded lovely and I had never been there before. I had had enough of London, the weather, the people, and I had burnt out in my job. I had been there for ten years and I had allowed my job to become my life and my identity, while working 24/7. I had piled on weight living off sugar and caffeine just to get through the day, I had no friends left, I had no life, my stress levels were at an all- time high, and I was trying to heal from a heart- wrenching breakup. I was a horrible person, terribly miserable, my life was being sucked out of me. It suddenly dawned on me that this was not life. I wanted more – life is for living, not for sitting in death's living room… So, I had put my plan into action. I gave notice to my boss and he wished me luck and said that he was sorry to see me go but understood. I went on my merry way. Two weeks later, I was called back into the office and offered an opportunity which changed the course of my life.

"Do you have a job in Vancouver?" my boss asked. "No," I replied.

"Do you have anywhere to live in Vancouver?" "No." "Do you know anyone in Vancouver?" "No."

"What do you plan to do?"

"I am not sure, I will just get there and then see," was my final answer. He said that he understood that I wanted to get out of London but did not want to lose me, so I was offered the opportunity to open an office in Europe. I decided the universe had put that in my path for a reason; I cancelled my Vancouver flight and bought a one-way ticket to Nice, France leaving in September.

I spent a year and a half in Europe. I had a great time, I got a life back, I made great lifelong friends, travelled, basked in the Mediterranean sunshine, and attempted to speak French. Unfortunately I swapped sugar and caffeine for champagne, wine and chocolate… Yes, you guessed it – I think I lost one pound and I think that was water weight as I drank more of that, too!

Although I loved my life in Europe, I felt the job was coming to an end and I wanted more. I bravely – or stupidly – decided to venture into the entrepreneurial world. I could not stay in Monaco as it was too expensive, so I sat in front of my computer and did a Google search – where should I live next? The top three cities came up as Vancouver, Sydney and Vienna. Vancouver did not feel right at that time, Sydney did not appeal, so hey, why not Vienna? I gave my notice in once more and had to give six months. In that time, I met a Croatian man who was so handsome. I thought that every single Christmas and birthday celebration had come my way. He then asked me to move to Croatia to live with him. I did not want to do a long-distance relationship, so I said yes. It was kind of 'make it or break it'.

I put all my stuff in storage, over-filled a car and set off on this new adventure with this man I had not known really for that long. Once there, I began Croatian classes, made friends, got to know his mother (who did not speak English but was lovely. She told him the way to keep me happy was to give me lots of orgasms and sex! Loved that woman.) Sadly, after three weeks he told me that it was not working, so I panic- bought Vienna, packed up my stuff and moved again two weeks later. I have spoken before about how when situations go smoothly, I feel that I am in alignment with where I should be in life. Well… it was a shit show from the moment I got to Vienna, but I fell in love with a flat and against my gut instinct, I signed up and moved in. I stayed for a year and a half. I adored my flat which was a home to me, and I had great friends, but I could not get residency. I went back to the South of France for three months to 'try before I buy', but that did not feel right either. Full circle, and I arrived back at booking a ticket to Vancouver, where the first phase of my book writing ends.

It is in Vancouver that I finish following in mum's footsteps. Mixed emotions swam around my body, knowing that the actual writing of this book will end and that it had taken over my life! However, I was so excited to think I can finally share it with you, the readers. I hoped my poverty would end and I could get a haircut… Oh, the dreams! Did I think about the future? For sure! However, the one thing I had learnt on my journey was to take one day at a time. I now know I have no control over my life!

02nd November 2019

I headed into Seattle to see what it had to offer. To be honest, the only thing I knew of Seattle was 'Grey's Anatomy' (which is filmed in LA of course) and the famous movie 'Sleepless in Seattle', so I was not really sure what I was going to do or see. I jumped on an express bus which rapidly took us all into the city. As I had no reference point, I closed my eyes and opened them, then got off at the next stop. It was on Pike Street which is very famous as it leads down to Pike Place Market – a very old market which opened in 1907 and is now a very large tourist trap. You can probably buy almost anything from the vast variety of stalls. The stuff being sold ranged from fruit and vegetables to honey, art, clothes, chintz for your home, along with anything and everything it seemed.

There was a fish stall where a lot of people were standing around not buying anything but with their mobiles out, seemingly waiting for something to happen, so of course I did the same. I heard murmurings that some singing was going to ensue. We waited for about 10 minutes, then the men running the fish stall started singing and throwing a fish around. It was quite a spectacle and delighted the crowd!

Whilst I was meandering through the hundreds of stalls, something came into my head and I realised I was in the city where it all began: The coffee shop movement! I headed off to find the first-ever Starbucks which opened its doors in 1971.

"This is where it all began.... My dream to build a company That fosters respect and dignity, To create a place where we can all come together over a cup of coffee"

-Howard Schutz

I feel like I either own a part of the company or at least I am an investor as I have spent so much money and time in Starbucks all over the world in different cities... Each have their own story to tell, changing but not changing with the needs of the times and customers. Having to compete with the next trendy coffee shop opening up down the road. People gather, deals are done, businesses formed and worked on, break ups, make ups and people sitting just to be around others or to be in the warmth. The green and white iconic sign on every street corner kind of makes you feel like home. There is a huge sense of familiarity when you enter a Starbucks. It was a modest place, obviously now a huge tourist trap but it was good to see it sitting in the busyness of the market. The queue was huge, and it was obviously higher priced than regular shops. The staff were great, and it felt personal. They managed to make me feel like not just another customer. Coffee finished, I found myself needing the restroom, so I found a plaza and used theirs. On the way back I was just about to go down an escalator (there were four or five different escalator options, but I took this one and I had to walk to it!) I am actually building up to a story which made me stop in my tracks and gave me a huge boost of confidence and a spring in my step. I have to just go back a few months. You know by now that I am a believer in signs and sometimes when I am feeling down, scared, or lacking in confidence, I ask for a sign that I am on the right path (as you know). I ask for either miracles (random things that make me smile) or I ask mum to send me something specific.

A few months back when I had just bought my ticket to LA, I asked mum to send me a sign that I was doing the right thing. I asked for her to send me a giraffe. The signs I ask for can manifest in many different ways – a picture, on a TV show, someone talking about one, a toy and or even a real one! I completely forgot about it, until this day. Just before I got on the escalator to go down, something caught my eye in the window of a gift shop. A china giraffe! I smiled to myself and walked over to the window with the face and enthusiasm of a child wowing in wonderment, seeing their favourite toy displayed in the shop window.

This was not just any giraffe, it was exactly the same giraffe that was in our family home, which sat proudly on a lamp table in our lounge. Since mum died and the house has gone, that giraffe came with me and has proudly sat in many different rooms, flats and countries. I have never seen one for sale before… I literally ran into the shop and startled the man behind the counter. I asked how much it was… I was in such awe and excitement that I was really not sure what to do with myself! I was not really interested in how much it was, but he picked it up and did not know as it did not have a price. I walked out with happy tears welling up. After that I went into a Cheesecake Factory, which was everywhere and is famous, so I thought whilst in Rome. The problem was that they put their calorie content next to each slice, so it put me off, clearly not too off as I still had one! I was totally underwhelmed by the one I chose – I knew I should have gone for chocolate… I am not the biggest fan of cheesecake anyway! At least I could tick it off my bucket list. I then headed home.

03rd November 2019

After waking I decided to go to a local coffee shop to do some writing. I wanted to try a contemporary one which looked like the trendy place for over 30-somethings to go on a Sunday morning, so I planted myself at table and soaked up the atmosphere. It was great to watch everyone. It was a different vibe from Starbucks, but I still managed to get a lot done. I sat there for a couple of hours before going back to my home to pack and get organised for my final bus journey.

Vancouver – The Beginning of the End

04th November 2019

My final bus trip! Crossing over the border into Canada I was nervous but excited. Are you one of those people that whenever you see police you instantly feel guilty or nervous as if you have to justify just walking Down the street? Even though you are a law abiding citizen? No? Just me? I was bought up to fear and respect the police, so I have this natural nervousness around them! Even though back in my 20s I married (and divorced) one! This is also me when coming up against border security! I have a clean record, I am not going to outstay my welcome, I have funds to support myself (albeit only a few), I am not smuggling anything, and I just want to visit but I am nervous! The bus itself had seen better days as I sat my pert bottom on ripped seat covers (who does that in the first place? Ripping I mean) but I was on the home stretch. I decided to watch the movie 'Eat Pray Love' inspired by the book by Elizabeth Gilbert, but I was only half watching. Though I am completely with her, I love to eat and pray for wine! The other half of the time watching the USA disappearing into the background and eagerly looking out for the first glimpses of Canadian life.

Of course, getting through the border was not an issue though it was worse than a job interview. I never know whether to smile and be bright and breezy or serious, so I am somewhere in between. I just smiled while looking like my hernia was hurting. I know they have to be tough in these times, but it was still a harrowing experience. Allowing the adrenaline to settle I checked my phone and realised it was not working. I couldn't get on the internet to see where I needed to go – adrenaline straight back up again, I felt like I was on a rollercoaster.

September 28th 1958

We left the motel at about 10 am. Our first lift was with a couple of Hungarian refugees who very kindly drove us all the way to Penticton even though they weren't going all that way. From there we hitched in the back of a van to Hedley and lastly all the rest of the way in a car with two very scruffy looking hunters. We were a bit doubtful about them, but they were quite decent. One of them was a funny character, one of them was the joking type. Gerrie and I both felt rather sick on the way. We put it down to the lack of food. Summertime daylight saving ended today so we had an extra hour on the way. We arrived into New Westminster at 6.30 am to a glorious sunset. The whole of the skyline was a deep red haze. From New Westminster we had to catch a bus into Vancouver. It was very difficult getting on with our packs.

VANCOUVER – THE BEGINNING OF THE END

04th November 2019

Then, of course I arrived with a plume of drama! After I got off the bus, I had to figure out how to get to my Airbnb – so pissed off that I could not use my phone for data, calls or texts. Luckily, I remembered that I had not cancelled my European sim card and so I switched that on knowing that with every minute it was costing me stupid money, but I had no choice!

I let my Airbnb host know that I was on my way and began my mission with my luggage to get to my 'home'. Whilst walking along I was approached by two different women asking if I wanted help… I really appreciated them asking and how nice it was. I was so embarrassed by the weight of the suitcases, I turned them down. It had almost become part of my journey to struggle with my luggage and maybe there was now a part of me that enjoyed the struggle… Who knows? (Have you ever thought about that? You could be addicted to suffering or the struggle? It becomes a part of your persona and identity? A little bit of psychology thrown in there.) I was nearing the apartment when suddenly this guy came up to me and started telling me he came to the station to meet me but could not find me – this was my host! How cute was that? He was probably hoping that this struggling, oversized luggage lady could not possibly be his tenant! Also, the photo of me on Airbnb is so much nicer than me right at that moment, with hair up, no makeup, glasses, looking like shit after a long journey.

We went to the Airbnb and – I had to laugh… The last twist to this tale. The place looked like social housing. Luckily, the carpet in the communal area was a swirly red colour so you could not see the filth and stains, but you could smell it. The fire door looked like it actually had been in a fire – it was either black with mould or smoke, not sure.

He helped me up with my luggage, with me behind him apologising about the weight. He said that he was used to it as his business is dealing with luggage every day! I did not pay much attention but when we got in the flat, oh dear... Umm... I distracted myself by chatting to the host, who was very friendly (my mind kept flashing back to Long Beach and the disgusting, pot-smoking frat house and the similarities!) We talked for ages and he told me that he only got in that day to sort things out. I was not sure whether to laugh or cry, so I held off but did mention that the bedroom smelt of smoke. It must have been from another flat, but I was hoping a whole lot of air freshener would help!

He eventually left and that was when inspector Sophie came out and I was horrified... There was black, toxic mould in the bathroom. I then looked around for more and it was in the living room too... Along with dust and dirt. I immediately texted him to tell him this and he came back and had a look. I told him that I could not stay there and dreaded the battle I was about to have with Airbnb to sort it out. Luckily, I was very fortunate that I had a good case worker who was sympathetic and helped out enormously. We both agreed I was to find a hotel for that one night, then work on finding the next month's home. When I was leaving, I met with my would-be neighbour. He asked me where I had come from and I told him that I was going to stay at the apartment but that I was no longer. He was a little frustrating to chat to as he did not understand what I was saying. He asked at one point if the reason I was leaving was because of his dogs... A huge red flag... He was an oddball... Another red flag... He needed a huge lock on his door... RUN, SOPHIE, RUN!

I found a place around the corner and off I went. This place was so cute – it was an apartotel. Very art deco and a writer's dream. When I arrived, I explained the fun that I had been having with the mould and the desk clerk was horrified telling me she had experience with mould once, and with bed bugs. She was very nice. I was so impressed by the people in Vancouver– friendly and helpful. This had made my experience so far a lot more pleasant and easier to deal with the crap I had encountered. I was given an executive suite, from where I was sure thrillers had been written.

It was the perfect ambiance along with a great view of Vancouver at night. It was a one-bedroom suite, so I had my own kitchen, dining and seating area with a separate bedroom. I loved it… I realised I had not eaten, so I went hunting for some food.

The area, the Westend, was lovely. Davies Street is vibrant, colourful, clean, safe and proud to be the gay capital of Vancouver. There were so many great-looking eateries and coffee shops, all serving different food, flavours and ambience, but with a relaxed look. I passed one in particular that got my attention, and it was the most adorable diner. I noted that I was to go back. I went into a supermarket, to just get food to-go. I picked out my food and went hunting for the wine section… I hunted and hunted, and eventually asked someone. He told me that supermarkets don't sell wine. Oh dear, golly gosh, I was going to be more sober than a detox patient. Then I heard the words, "But there is a liquor store around the corner." Music to my ears and a zinging to my taste buds! I went to the liquor store which was surprising and not full of alcoholics with their brown paper bags and $5 rocket fuel. I noticed the prices for wine and again, the realisation that my liver was going to love me hits me in the face... It was so expensive... I found a bottle which was not extortionate and went back to my hotel.

I spent the evening looking for a new place to live but I was so tired that I ate my food, had one glass of wine and went to bed, thinking to myself that mum and the girls did not always have success with where they stayed either

September 28th 1958

In Vancouver we went straight to the Y only to be told there were no vacancies. However, they recommended a place nearby called Ailsa Lodge. We lugged all our luggage over and booked a room for three. Ailsa Lodge was exactly like a rest home for old people. They were all sitting in the lounge watching TV when we arrived. We just dumped everything and then went in search of food. We went into two places and then out again because they were too expensive. Finally, we found a smoky German restaurant where we had a very good meal, cheap. I had liver for the proteins. It was a nice little place with loads of atmosphere. We sat on stools at the counter. The other two were so dizzy they thought they would fall off. We again went to bed pretty early.

05th November 2019

The next morning, I wanted to speak to the manager of the apartotel to see if I could negotiate a monthly rate and stay there. He was exactly as I had imagined – large belly, huge gold chain, no interest in helping out, so I checked out and left.

Instead I managed to find somewhere else, with Airbnb's help, but I figured out that downtown Vancouver was way out of my budget to get somewhere decent to live. You either seem to get the amazing apartment inside but dodgy area outside, or the dodgy inside and great area outside, unless you want to spend big bucks. I decided on decent both, but in the suburbs. I was tired of settling on where I lived but I had to be realistic. I was a little disappointed, but I knew this was all for a reason, to keep on smiling and entertaining you guys. After checking out I had that lull between checking out and checking into my new Airbnb, so I decided to head to that diner which caught my eye the night before. It is called 'Mary's on Davie' and it was brimming with cuteness. It is an American Diner straight from 'Grease' the movie, inspired from the 60s but certainly with a modern twist. It has the colours, the booths, the breakfast bar, the lovely staff and I am sure it sparkles. When I walked in, I was overwhelmed by where to sit. Do I sit in a comfortable booth on a high table to people watch, or at the bar which was special! I loved it... I opted for sitting on a high table to people watch and happily sat there drinking drip coffee thinking this was probably what mum did all those years ago. Drinking drip coffee in a diner and writing.

I left the diner, though I could have stayed for the whole day... And jumped in a taxi to get to my next home. I said goodbye to the city and found myself in death valley where nobody goes! For these last few weeks, I wanted to be in the hub, the noise, the bright lights and life. I wanted to feel the energy of the city and those who lived, worked or visited there. I had been on my own for so long that I wanted to go to meetups and be with others as my journey came to an end, but the taxi was taking me further and further away from all of that.

I arrived at my new place and it was lovely. It was clean, I had the whole little flat to myself, but it was so quiet. No hum of cars, sirens or people, only the sound of my anger rising inside of me. I got angry that I was in a situation where I could not afford to stay in the city, that my choices were limited, and the whole overall fucking situation. I resented the book and the universe, I wanted so badly to say fuck it, go to a hotel or a better Airbnb in the city, and put it on a credit card. I wanted to scream! In those moments I have choices, I can either go into a 'poor me, I am a victim' mode or put my big girl pants on and get out there. So, I went in search of life. It did not get much better.

The nearest sign of civilisation within walking distance was pretty grotty, cheap shops that were not well looked after but I kept going, hoping to find the diamond in the ruff. I passed a salon who advertised to get my eyebrows done. I desperately needed them tinting so I went in and asked how much. When she told me, it was very reasonable, she invited me to sit down, so I did. After many minutes of her chatting to someone else she came over and started preparing my eyebrows. Nervously, I told her what I wanted, and hoped and prayed that they would turn out okay. I was thinking how I would look having to shave them all off if I had to… She seemed to know what she was doing so I lay back and closed my eyes!

"Oh… You are beauuuuutiful ladeeeee,"she said in a Persian accent.

"Oh, thank you," I said to myself! "You have such beauuuuutiful eyelashes and skin."

"Yes," I said to myself…

"Oh, you are beauuuuutiful, so lucky," she continued. "Keep going," I said to myself. I felt very special and thought, "Well, thank you, I am flattered!"

She said this a few more times, boosting my ego some more, until she had put the tint on and needed it to set, so she went into the back room where someone else was waiting for a treatment. I was lying on the chair and suddenly I hear coming from the other room,

"Oh… you are beauuuuuutiful ladeeeee. Oh, you are beauuuuuutiful, so lucky."

What the fuck? My ego deflated as I giggled to myself… Not so special now, huh? I think back to what my mum said about the mina bird on Catalina Island… I get it, MUM!

"There were some lovely birds there but the most interesting were the Mina birds. They all had a long repertoire, one even wolf whistled. We were quite flattered until we realised what it was!"

My eyebrows turned out how I wanted them, phew… I got to keep them! I said goodbye and kept on walking. The cloud in which I arrived under was unfortunately still there as I walked around not finding that diamond. So, I got some bits and pieces of food and headed back to the flat.

06th November 2019

Despite waking up, still with the anger, resentment and annoyance, I decided to try to get out of it by going on an exploratory walk of the area. I know I was not going to find the 'life' I was wanting but I may have missed something. I walked down to the waterside and instantly knew how a prisoner on Alcatraz felt looking across the water at the people having fun and a life whilst I was stuck in a 'prison'. I know, I know, that is dramatic but looking at the city from where I was did not help lift my mood. So, Ispent the rest of the day watching TV and chatting to a friend.

07th November 2019

Right, stop now – this was getting ridiculous. If the city could not come to me, I would go to the city. On a bus I jumped, landing in Vancouver city. I stopped at the biggest Starbucks I have ever been in, to do some research of where I needed to go, and to have a coffee. The atmosphere was great, and it was very well organised for the busyness of the place. Bankers, office workers, remote workers and locals all made up the audience. I then continued on my mission of seeing where mum and the girls went, I walked a little up the road to a cheap clothes store wondering if I should stock up on a warmer wardrobe. I gathered a few jumpers off the rails and went into the dressing room where it had the dreaded mirrors which show you from all angles. "Oh…" is all I could say when I took off my jumper. The lights and mirror were showing me every new lump and bump, wobbly bit, extra lb, oh and a few stray hairs on my chin! Bollocks, I get it… Of course, I vowed there and then not to eat anything over 100 calories in a sitting, and to start walking my 10,000 steps a day (let's not get too carried away with jogging!) I put my mindset into action and visualised that I was slimmer. I almost threw the discarded large sized clothes at the assistant and mumbled, "No thanks," marching out with vigour and determination. I went to the places where mum mentioned she went and of course, a huge sign of the times means that they had either been pulled down to make way for new developments or there was no sign of what was there before. However, I loved that sense I got, pounding the same streets I know mum had done. Robson Street, Dunsmuir Street, Melville Street and Burrard Street, to name a few. Ailsa Lodge was now a development site. I also stumbled upon the Georgia

Hotel which appeared to not have changed the exterior.

Although YMCA's were usually strictly for men, others welcomed families and women to stay. It was mum's equivalent to my Airbnbs. I think Vancouver has a lovely feel, relaxed but visionary, caters for the professional very well. It is like a chameleon catering for the winter and summer crowd as the ski slopes are a stone's throw away. I can understand when people say – once you come, you never leave. Mum, I know, loved it. The darker side of Vancouver can be found on Main Street by East Hastings where the drug addicts seemed to gather, but I do not think mum had that problem when she was there or certainly not the same extent.

I arrived back to the warmth of my flat and I thought to myself that I had been so good not eating anything 'bad' for at least four hours, I rewarded myself with a doughnut! Ha ha… Just kidding, it was actually a very large glass of red wine!

September 29th 1958

Next morning, we ate a picnic breakfast in our room. We ate our cornflakes out of glasses and crushed up lumps of sugar. Gerrie rang up Bob Vowells who said he would be around at 11.00am. We waited for him in the lounge amongst the aspiditras. Bob was very helpful about accommodation and suggested staying in housekeepers' rooms. He drove us to one or two until we found one that suited us. It was on Robson Street (1506). We paid $15.00 for the room which was $5.00 each for the week. The landlady put an extra bed in for us. We could see the water from our window. Also, we weren't very far from Stanley Park. There was a separate communal kitchen and bathroom. The place was very shabby, but it was sufficient for us.

Bob drove us to the main shopping area then left us. First, we went to the Mexican Consulate where Gerrie and I got out visas. Janet hasn't even got her passport so we don't know whether or not she will be able to go. There was a fabulous view of the city from the office. Next, we went to see about insurance. It all seemed too expensive that I decided to leave it and think about it. One of the agents was from Esher whose parents knew Lulu and Eileen – it's a small world! Walking around Vancouver we met Joan and Lucy (two English sisters, chambermaids).

We had a natter and they told us that all the unemployed Banff met at the Honeydew on Granville and Dunsmuir at 12.00pm and 5.00pm. So, we went at 12.00pm. There we met Ann, Pat and Vera and another girl. It was so nice seeing them again. We also went back again at 5.00pm. We called in at the Georgia Hotel to see if Andre was there, but he wasn't. Bob said he would pick us up at 10.00pm so we had supper then wrote letters, etc. until then. He took us on a tour of the city through Stanley Park to the British Properties where we got a bird's eye view of the city. We finally got it through to him that we were hungry, so he immediately took us to a drive-in for half a chicken. It was the first drive- in we had been to. He then drove us back. We sat in the car and talked for at least two hours, so it was pretty late when we finally go in. I bought myself a pair of desert boots in Kelowna. I look pretty awful in them, but they are sturdy.

I Fucking Made it!

09th November 2019

I finally made it! I followed in my mum's footsteps as much as I could. There have, of course, been decisions made of not doing some things due to time or money constraints but what I had achieved, I was pretty bloody proud of myself.

I woke up and jumped on a bus in order to go to Stanley Park and see some other parts of Vancouver that mum and the girls had done. As I got off the bus my body seemed to be screaming at me in annoyance that I had not stayed in bed. My bones ached, I could not stop yawning and my legs, well they are heavy anyway, but boy did they feel so much heavier! So, I found the Starbucks I was in the other day and went and ordered a very large coffee.

The guy behind the counter asked how I was doing, and I think he regretted it as I started to babble on about wanting to be in bed and gave him a five-minute tale of how I was feeling. His eyes had glazed over, the smile had gone and the panic on his face had given it all away. When I paused to take a breath, he took the opportunity by asking the next person what they wanted so I skulked away, grabbed my coffee and sat down.

The vibe was totally different. It was Sunday morning locals. I sat and watched until I felt the need to get up and go. The more I walked the more my body came back to me, though it was cold. Boy, was I hoping that it was going to be worth it. I walked via the marina and the people completely changed. They became affluent and you could literally smell the money. The small cute dogs were out by the dozen. There was one being walked by the housekeeper and he was a small white thing. They stopped and the dog got up on its back paws and begged for a snack. It was wearing a sparkly bow tie and I watched, thinking to myself, "Ah, how cute…" He took the snack then literally went for me! He was yanked back by the lead luckily otherwise I would have had my ankles done for! Bloody hell, I walked a little faster.

I got to Stanley Park and saw that they had a horse drawn tour of the park. So, I did some quick maths in my head and decided to do it. It took about an hour and was cold despite having a blanket. It was interesting and I got to see the park, the Lion's Gate Bridge, the British Properties and the Lost Lagoon, all which mum had seen and commented on. Even though they were quick glimpses today, I thought that I could go back another time.

After the ride, I made up my mind and went to the movies as I had not been for such a long time. There, I could lose myself in magic, love and romance. I decided to see 'Last Christmas' which is a great film and of course I get caught up in it all and want my life to have a happy ending! I then head back with warm fuzzy feelings. A great day, to a great end.

I would like to have gone to Victoria, people have told me it is very quaint and different to Vancouver – I will get there one day. I do know I will NOT be going over the Calipo Bridge as mum did. Mum was so much braver than I am – I prefer to be on sturdy ground, as I hate heights! I will bid a fond farewell here.

Mum and the girls had many more adventures in and around Vancouver – I shall let them tell you about it.

September 30th 1958

Up at 11.00am and into town again to meet at the Honeydew. The three Welsh girls were also there. Then we wandered around. I got my insurance at Cooks ($8.10) and also a record for Carol's 21st and souvenirs. Went for a walk along the docks. Back for a supper of pork chops after which we sat talking for at least an hour to people from Banff. Then we wrote diaries and letters till 11.00pm.

October 01st 1958

We had a busy day today. We set off fairly early on the bus for Cleveland Dam. Just as we were changing buses, a lady behind offered to take us the rest of the way in her car. Then we hitched to the suspension bridge, it was very precarious and unsafe. Next door was a private garden made into a jungle with stuffed wild animals in it and painted boughs and branches made to look like insects. It was quite interesting.

From there we hitched to Stanley Park. We walked a short way to Prospect Point, a lovely place. There was a large totem pole with the Lion's Gate Bridge in the background. We had a snack in the restaurant there. We hitched right to the park to the zoo and rose gardens. I collected quite a few different coloured Maple leaves for my scrap book. Some of the trees looked so lovely with their fall colouring. The zoo was a very clean one. We sat on a bank by the Lost Lagoon for about half an hour glorying in our freedom and good fortune. From there we took about three buses out to UBC. It was a wonderful place. It seemed far too grand for a university. It must be a pleasure to work there. We had a light supper as Bob was taking us out at 10.00. He took us to a Chinese restaurant called The Forbidden City. It was pretty empty, but it was a good meal. We each had one dance with Bob. He plays in a band and quite fancies his dancing. We were asked to leave before the cabaret, so we had another runaround in the car. We were supposed to be leaving in the morning for Seattle via Victoria, but Bob persuaded us to stay until Sunday night when he would drive us down. We said no at first but then decided it would be cheaper and would be less trouble. He again talked for ages in the car.

October 02nd 1958

Walked down to the Ferry at the docks at 11.00am. The water was as calm as a millpond. Unfortunately, it was rather misty, but it cleared quite a bit. We sat out on the deck with our shoes off and lounging in the sun until we left the sheltered bay then we had to go inside. We went underneath the Lion's Gate Bridge so got a worm's eye view of it. The journey took us about two and a quarter hours. We all fell asleep towards the end.

We landed at Nanaiamo and decided to hitch to Victoria. We walked up through the quay until we came to a large square structure which had housed the world's biggest birthday cake for the B.C. Centennial. Unfortunately, it was in the process of being dismantled and all that was left was large crumbs of icing and the boards. A man called to us and offered us samples of the cake. We didn't need asking twice and each of us took a large handful thinking he meant we could eat the whole plate. He looked very shocked and told us not to make a meal of it! He gave us pieces of four-month old dusty icing which wasn't much consolation. I sent home the sample about as big as my finger for the novelty.

We arrived on our way up through the town on to the road to Victoria. It was too far to walk right out of the city limits, so we hitched in front of the houses. I hate hitchhiking anywhere there are people as they always stare and laugh. We got a short lift out of the town and then a second right to Victoria. Victoria is roughly 70 miles away and takes about one and a half hours. Our second lift was with a very nice boy who played in the Navy band. He was very helpful and took us into Victoria via the barracks which was the largest and most modern in Canada. He took us to the Y where we were told there was no room. They redirected us to a lovely little cottage opposite where we got a room for two. We dumped our luggage and went out in search of an English tea. We eventually found a place and had crumpets and coffee plus some delicious cakes we had bought in another shop. As Victoria is so English, we thought we would conform with the rest.

We walked down to the docks to the Parliament Buildings. It was dark by then and they looked really effective outlined in little lights. I tried taking my first time-exposure photo. Next, we looked around the Empress Hotel. Many things were similar to Banff. When we were on our way back, I discovered I had lost my menu (I have a mania for souvenirs), so I retraced my steps and luckily found it. We sat in the Y for about an hour reading magazines until we were nearly asleep and then went to bed. I don't know which I like best, Vancouver or Victoria. I should like to settle in both of them.

October 03rd 1958

Gerrie and I got up for breakfast at the Y. It was a good breakfast at a reduced rate. We decided to hitch out to the Butchart Gardens. We were very glad we didn't have the trouble of carting all our packs around. We just had a small bag each. We walked quite a way until we found a suitable hitching spot.

Our first lift didn't take us very far but our second turned out very well. It was a man with two small kids. He loved talking and eventually asked us if we would like to have lunch at his house. We accepted gladly. They were in the middle of moving and his wife had two more small kids, one nearly three weeks old. What she must have thought when he suddenly arrived with three girls for lunch, I cannot imagine! However, she managed and looked pleased.

They had a small cottage near the lake right out in the country. It was a lovely spot surrounded by trees, so peaceful. We helped a little with the lunch but there wasn't too much we could do. Mr Kelly showed us around the garden (or rather open plot) and then we just sat in the sun and played with the kids. Lunch was a very squashed one but delicious. There were six of us in a tiny room. The kids had to eat in a separate room and crawl under the table to get out. The three of us washed up afterwards. Patsy, the eldest child, aged five, took us into the garden again and between them she and her father gave us apples, beets, carrots, potatoes, cucumbers and beans all home grown produce. There were three large bags full, so Mr Kelly kindly offered to drop them at the Y for us to pick up later. The whole family were so nice to us, we couldn't get over it.

At about 3.00pm Mr Kelly drove us to the gardens. We were very sorry to say goodbye to them. We were a bit late for the gardens and only had time for a quick look around. It was well worth it ($1.10) however, they were so beautifully set out, a sunken garden and *rose garden, a Japanese garden, lawns, nurseries, paths, everything. Being such a beautiful day helped. We hitched back to the Y and picked up our belongings then caught a bus to the main highway. We got a lift with a boy called Art who was so typically American he made us laugh, really fast living. He wasn't going right into Nanaimo but when he reached his destination, he decided to take us on and return. He bought us supper on the way which was very nice of him. We felt a bit guilty as we met a girl from Banff in the ferry waiting room and while we were talking to her he left. We caught the 9.00am ferry back, 'The Princess of Nanaimo', the same one we came on.*

We were troubled on the way by some sailors who woke us up, so we foiled them and retired to the ladies' room. On arriving back in Vancouver, we had a real surprise by being met by Bob. We certainly weren't expecting him. Janet was so surprised she dropped the apples all over the floor! He took us to a drive-in where we only had room for pie and coffee then he drove us back. He really is here! We certainly are lucky with our lifts. Three meals paid for us today.

October 04th 1958

We stayed in bed till 11.00. Gerrie and I decided to go and get the shopping. Just as we were going up the road, we heard some yelling from a house opposite and discovered it was Ann, Pat and Vera. What a coincidence! The whole of Vancouver and we have to live almost opposite. We went up and had a chat then they walked us to the stores. We had a vegetable lunch from the Kellys. it took us ages to prepare. The three girls came over after lunch and stayed 'til 5.00pm talking. The day seemed to just fly past. Bob was picking us up at 7.30pm so we got ready. I wore my low black top and red skirt. He was late again as usual, but I was quite glad as I wouldn't have been ready anyway. He took us up the Grouse Mountain chair lift. We palmed him off on Gerrie with the excuse that she didn't like heights! The chair lift went up in two stages. The first one was okay but the second creaked so much that I honestly thought our chair was going to drop off. I was just like jelly when I got to the top! The view from the top gave me an extraordinary feeling as though we were looking down from the heavens, we were detached from the rest of the world. Luckily it was very clear evening. We had dinner in the chalet up there. A lovely log cabin lit by candlelight with a huge open fire at one end. There was a very friendly little band consisting of a pianist and a double base.

We all ordered steaks but when Bob was out, we decided they were too expensive and changed the order to chicken in a basket. I don't think he was too pleased when he got back! We had a few photos taken both in the chalet and on the way down in the chair lift. It was a lovely dinner. Coming down the chair lift seemed much faster and more enjoyable as we were facing the view. When we got down it was too late to go dancing as Bob had planned so he took us to a birthday party at a house. The party was almost over but the food was still plentiful (after a big meal too!) I danced with a boy and the other two went to sleep as Bob disappeared into the kitchen.

We had our usual long chat outside in the car. Bob really is an odd bod. He spends his time telling us what fine girls we are! I am beginning to wonder if he is sincere. Janet refused to play maracas at the chalet so that he could take a photo of her. He seems quite stuck on her though he tries not to show it.

October 05th 1958

Not up until 12.00. Had another vegetable lunch. Went over to say goodbye to the girls and took them a box of vegetables we couldn't finish. Didn't stay long as we had to get on with our packing. Bob rang up to say he would call for us at 3.30pm instead of 7.30pm so we had to rush but, in the end, he didn't turn up until 5.00. We saw the girls setting off on a walk, so we had another chat on the front porch.

"Dear Mummy and Daddy,

I am writing this from Vancouver. I found it in a book and as it already had a Canadian stamp on it, I thought I had better send it. At the moment, we are sitting waiting for Bob to come and pick us up to take us to Seattle. I am dying to get into the States. We have so much to see. This mountain was just by the hotel. It was one of my favourite ones. The weather has been perfect ever since we left Banff. Apparently, there has been an Indian Summer all along the Pacific coast. I hope it keeps up! It was 101 degrees in Los Angeles yesterday. Vancouver is a lovely city. The downtown shopping area has very wide roads and is well planned. The city seems more or less cut in half with calm blue water and hills and mountains stretching up beyond. We are staying on the opposite side to the mountains so from where I am sitting now in our room it looks just like Monte Carlo with houses dotted up the hillside. The houses here seem very modernistic and there is one area called British Properties where every house seems to have a swimming pool and a boat.

Fondest love Annabella"

When Bob finally picked us up, we piled everything into the car. He called into his house to drop somethings including some parcels we had given to him to post. Crafty! We left Vancouver in the blaze of another glorious sunset. Every single night there was one. We had dinner at King Neptune's in New Westminster, a seafood place. Bob's last fling. During the dinner he let it out that he had been married and divorced in seven months.

It was then we began to find out his true character. How hard and merciless he could be and more than ever what an oddball he was. He carried on talking and explaining all the way to Seattle so that by the time we got there we all felt really scared of him. We even wondered if he had a loudspeaker wired in his car and were really worried as we had been talking about him when we were alone.

When Gerrie and I went into the Y to see about booking he told Janet it was really her he liked (we had known all along). We had a hot chocolate before he left at 1.00. We were really glad to see the last of him even though he had been so good to us. We were all a bit apprehensive when coming through the customs in case they should query our packs, but we didn't have any trouble. Going to bed that night we really had the feeling of being in a different country. Poor Janet had nightmares over Bob!

What Happened Next

Mum, Gerrie and Janet end their adventures in Phoenix after going to the immigration service to extend their stay in the US. They were told that they did not have the right visas and that they were illegally in the country. They were given a few days to leave the country under 'DEPORTATION'.

Mum being mum in all her glory, decided to flirt a little with the immigration officer and ask him for a couple more weeks as goodbye parties would be thrown and they could not possibly let anyone down. This worked and they used the last couple of weeks for fond farewells before taking a bus back to Toronto.

February 06th 1959

"Dear Mummy and Daddy,

This shows the type of bus we travelled on. We sat on the back seat of the raised portion surround by air force guys. I had a nice comfortable one to lean on most of the way! About every two or three hours we would stop at one of these Greyhound bus stations for about 15 minutes. Every now and then they would stop for 30 minutes to an hour and would make everyone get out while they serviced the bus. Then they would pinch our pillows and we'd have to 'buy new ones'. We hid them one time, but they found them, the rats!

I'm writing this having breakfast with Gerrie in a restaurant in St Louis.

Fondest Love Annabella"

February 07th 1959

"Dear Rodney,

This is the bus we travelled from Phoenix to Toronto on. We changed at St Louis, Chicago and Detroit. They were very comfortable and even have washrooms on board. We spent a day and a night in St Louis, Missouri. We took a tour of the city in the afternoon then met someone who took us around in the evening. The next morning, we walked down and had a look at the might Mississippi River. We saw one of the paddle- steamers.

Give this to mum.

Love Annabella"

This was the last postcard and the real end to her journey. She stayed in Toronto until the end of April 1959 when she then went back to the UK, just in time to celebrate her 21st Birthday. Gerrie remained in Toronto and subsequently met her ex-husband. As for Janet, not a lot is known about her. Mum and Gerrie's friendship grew and grew and they became very good friends. I had the pleasure to still be her friend and we would laugh and cry when we think and talk about mum.

The experiences they shared formed this unbreakable bond and the fact they had to rely on each other whilst still trying to get to know each other, was very brave. Their love for adventure kept them going and their sociability and friendliness, along with their fascinating story, allowed them to experience so much more and meet incredible people. Their free spirits, courage and youth intrigued their hosts and drivers and now they are fascinating you, the readers

An article written by Huddersfield Weekly Examiner, Saturday, December 13, 1958

The Way of Adventure

The modern girl is as adventurous as any boy when it comes to striking out in travel. This week I have been hearing something of the journeys of Miss Annabella Bisiker, daughter to Mr and Mrs T.D. Bisiker of Surrex House, Stanwell Avenue. A year ago, twenty-year-old Miss Bisiker, a former Waverly schoolgirl, was working in an office in Toronto. Then she decided to see as much of the New World as she could. In the space of six months' travel in the West she has visited Vancouver, San Francisco, Hollywood, Mexico and is now in Arizona, where she has a temporary post in a hotel in a town called Phoenix. But she is getting ready to move on again, and plans to visit Florida, cross the seas to Jamaica and then trek back to Toronto.

Ghost Town

In California Miss Bisiker visited Calico, the ghost town that came back. For long years Calico boomtown of the silver mines, lay dead. Then it was revived as a show place where moderns could see how the old- timers lived. In the ghost town grill the visitor can partake of pioneer beef stew, 1.25,"cooked as the miners liked it in the days of '49" with boysenberry tart and ice cream to follow, 30c. then he can go round the to the office of the "Ghost Town News" and have his name printed on the front page of the day's newspaper, as Annabella did.

Millions of people visit Ghost Town every year. Guess it wishes sometimes it was a ghost town again.

I often think to myself how I have transformed from taking this journey, but I think that is the wrong word to use – it should be how did I survive this journey? The answer is simple – with carbs, sugar and red wine!

Jokes aside, I have faced insurmountable fear, mostly around my financial situation but also not having a lot of self-belief that this is my destiny and purpose. My head has said so many times, "What are you doing? Get on a flight back to the UK and get a job!" But my spirit and gut instinct said to keep going. Listening to the inner belief that this story is meant to be shared and told has given me courage and strength between the moments of fear. Having the signs from mum and the universe have given me comfort in the lonely times.

Kindness and support have come from unexpected places. I have found myself with people and in situations I never would have thought I would be in or tolerated before. My five-star life was a distant memory and I have had to dig deep for resilience, courage and kick in my survival instinct. I was reminded by one of my brothers on a phone call that the lack of money was part of my journey and if I had money, my experiences would certainly not have been as juicy, heart wrenching or even funny. Though, the lack of money certainly took away choices.

"Ruin is the Road to Transformation" - Elizabeth Gilbert

I have talked a lot about the homeless and drugs on the streets and how shocked I am by it. It has had a huge impact on me. How easy it is for people to fall into being on the streets. It is not necessarily that they were drug addicts or alcoholics before – they are just people who had homes, cars, families, jobs and a life, but circumstances have put them out. I have met these people and they really are treated like outcasts or ghosts. Some turn to drugs and alcohol to cope.

This is probably the proudest lesson I have learnt, to not judge and show more compassion of people who I do not understand or would have feared, as that kept me in my bubble. I do not like to see people openly taking drugs, I do not like the smell of the unkempt, but ignoring it will not make it go away. They need kindness and compassion. The one advantage that the homeless have over housed people I have noticed, is that they have a community. I saw them gathered on the streets chatting away to each other, maybe it is the old adage, people come together in times of need – or is it the drugs? I have learnt that to be a true adventurer you have to go out of your comfort zone. Learning to surrender and realise I have no control over my life has been an eye opener. I have let go even more of the perfection and I now take one day at a time. Whatever happens

I will be okay and I will find my happy ending. I am becoming visible – I am okay with that and now I know 'A life beyond Fear is a life with Freedom'.

The End… For now!

Thank You

These thanks go to the people behind the scenes!
First off, I must thank my mentor and editor, who without her I would have jumped off that ledge! Samantha Worthington, you are a star!

Of course, I must say a huge thanks to my brothers. Jules your support has been incredible and thanks to you and Babs for being my number one fans. Tim, thanks for some wise words and the tremendous support you gave me which helped me through, and Mark, a huge thank you.

Then come my VIP supporters, who, without them I would not have been able to manage all my travel: Rachel Whittlesey Burnett, Rafael Navarro – Thanks for believing in me.

Thanks to my anonymous donors and also to Marie and Samuel, huge appreciation of your support.

To my spiritual coach who has been with me on a much larger journey for a few years and helped me believe in the universe again – Erica, keep shining and spreading your magic.

Linda, friend, supporter, super star and SFguide.

Ina, Franck, and of course Mr V.(Valentin)– Love you guys. To 'Janet' wherever you are – thank you.

Thank you, Leslie for the acting classes.

Thanks to Sharyn for helping me when I needed it.

Thanks to Ruben for checking up on me throughout my travels. To those places that allowed me to sit for hours writing.

I thank the universe for sending me on this journey and putting me in a pile of shit financially – as I would not have had the adventures I did and learnt what I have.

Gerrie, you were incredible, and we have agreed many times that you were such an amazing friend to mum. She was so lucky to have you in her life and it has been a privilege to write this story.

UPDATE - Sadly Gerrie passed away, but she will always be in my thoughts and heart.

Thank you for the gift – keep sending me those signs.

Over and Out.

www.ingramcontent.com/pod-product-compliance
Lightning Source LLC
Chambersburg PA
CBHW070426010526
44118CB00014B/1916